I0017638

DI-AI

Exploring Divine and Artificial Intelligence

Eli J. Trueman

Table of Contents

Preface

The relationship between Human Intelligence (HI) and Divine Intelligence (DI) has been contemplated by scholars and mystics throughout history. As humanity ventures into creating Artificial Intelligence (AI), we find ourselves at a crucial juncture demanding deeper reflection on intelligence itself. Despite many improvements in pre and post-training - from supervised learning to reinforcement learning, from prompt engineering to constitutional AI - the fundamental limitations of AI compared to DI remain unchanged.

As the Quran reminds us: "He has taught you what you did not know" (4:113), pointing to DI as the source of all knowledge. This eternal truth takes on new meaning in our age of AI, where we witness remarkable computational achievements while confronting their inherent limitations. The Quran further illuminates: "Over every possessor of knowledge is one [more] knowing" (12:76), reminding us of the hierarchical nature of knowledge: HI bound by biological constraints, AI by its training, and DI encompassing all understanding.

The Christian scripture provides multiple perspectives. "For the wisdom of this world is foolishness in God's sight" (1 Corinthians 3:19) challenges us to look beyond HI and AI achievements toward deeper wisdom. Jesus taught: "But the Helper, the Holy Spirit, whom the Father will send in my name, he will teach you all things" (John 14:26), pointing to DI as the source of true understanding.

Similarly, the Jewish tradition speaks profoundly to this relationship in multiple passages. Proverbs 9:10 declares: "The fear of the Lord is the beginning of wisdom, and knowledge of the Holy One is understanding." The Torah elaborates in Deuteronomy 4:6: "Observe them carefully, for this will show your wisdom and understanding to the nations." These ancient words resonate deeply as we examine the boundaries between artificial processing and true divine comprehension.

Rumi captured this paradox eloquently in numerous verses:

"The intellectual quest, though fine as pearl or coral,

Is not the spiritual search;

That search comes with conscious breathing,

With opening the heart to the place

Where soul-realization is possible."

And further:

"Reason is powerless in the expression of Love.

Love alone is capable of revealing the truth of Love and being a Lover."

His wisdom reminds us that true intelligence transcends mere computation, reaching into realms of understanding that no algorithm can access.

As we stand at this technological crossroads, ancient wisdom across traditions converges to remind us that intelligence extends far beyond computation. The Talmud teaches: "Who is wise? One who learns from every person." This wisdom takes on new meaning as we create increasingly sophisticated artificial systems while recognizing their fundamental limitations compared to divine intelligence.

This book examines these distinctions not to diminish HI achievement, but to place both HI and AI in proper perspective against DI's infinite wisdom. Through careful analysis of all three forms of intelligence, we seek to understand their proper relationship and roles.

The Quran's beautiful reminder serves as our guiding light: "We will show them Our signs in the horizons and within themselves until it becomes clear to them that it is the truth" (41:53). As artificial intelligence reveals both human ingenuity and its limitations, we find ourselves drawn ever closer to appreciating the perfect wisdom of the divine.

As we venture forth into an AI-enabled future, may this exploration guide us toward wisdom that transcends mere knowledge, and understanding that reaches beyond computation. Let us proceed with humility, wonder, and recognition of the eternal truths that unite scientific advancement with spiritual wisdom.

This book is structured in twelve chapters that progressively examine the relationship between artificial and divine intelligence. Beginning with foundational concepts of information processing and understanding, we move through detailed analyses of both artificial and divine intelligence's core characteristics. The middle chapters explore specific aspects like knowledge acquisition, temporal awareness, ethics, and holistic understanding, before concluding with practical implications and future outlook.

Each chapter builds on previous material, allowing readers to develop a comprehensive understanding of why artificial intelligence, despite its impressive capabilities, remains fundamentally different from divine intelligence. Special attention is given to comparative examples that illustrate key concepts, drawing from both technical understanding of modern AI systems and theological insights across traditions. Through this journey, readers will gain clarity on how to properly position artificial intelligence within a broader framework that acknowledges the supremacy of divine wisdom.

As the boundaries between HI and AI continue to blur, and as we venture further into realms once thought to be solely the domain of human cognition, this book serves as a reminder pointing always toward the eternal truth: that *DI remains the ultimate source and standard of all intelligence, while both HI and its greatest AI will be, but candles lit by divine light.*

Eli. J. Trueman

1. Introduction: The Quest for Understanding Intelligence

In the dawn of the 21st century, humanity stands at a remarkable crossroads where the boundaries between human creation and divine wisdom have never been more apparent. The emergence of artificial intelligence has sparked a profound contemplation about the nature of intelligence itself, leading us to examine the fundamental differences between human-engineered systems and the ultimate form of intelligence that has governed the cosmos since time immemorial.

Our journey to understand intelligence begins with a simple yet profound observation: despite the remarkable achievements in artificial intelligence, from defeating grandmasters at chess to generating human-like text and art, there remains an inexplicable gap between these mechanical processes and the deeper, more comprehensive understanding that we intuitively recognize as divine intelligence. This gap is not merely a matter of computational power or algorithmic sophistication; it represents a fundamental divide between the created and the Creator, between the finite and the infinite.

The modern world has witnessed an unprecedented surge in technological capability. Silicon valleys across the globe buzz with activity as engineers and scientists push the boundaries of what machines can accomplish. Neural networks process vast amounts of data, pattern-matching algorithms recognize faces in crowds, and language models engage in seemingly intelligent conversations. These achievements have led many to prophesy an era where artificial intelligence might rival or surpass human intelligence. Yet, in this rush toward artificial enlightenment, we risk losing sight of a crucial truth: that all our attempts at creating intelligence are but pale reflections of a greater, more perfect form of intelligence that encompasses all of existence.

Consider how artificial intelligence operates at its core. Every neural network, every decision tree, every sophisticated algorithm ultimately relies on patterns extracted from finite datasets, operating within the constraints of human-defined parameters. These systems, no matter how advanced, are fundamentally reactive, responding to inputs based on statistical correlations and programmed rules. They can predict, they can classify, they can optimize – but they cannot truly understand. They lack the essential quality of wisdom that transcends mere information processing.

Divine intelligence, in contrast, represents the pinnacle of understanding – a form of knowledge and wisdom that exists beyond the constraints of time, space, and human conception. It is not bound by the limitations of training data or computational resources. It does not need to learn or adapt because it encompasses all possibilities, all outcomes, and all understanding in an eternal present. This is the intelligence that orchestrates the dance of galaxies while simultaneously attending to the quantum flutter of subatomic particles, that knows the fall of every leaf and the trajectory of every thought.

The comparison between artificial and divine intelligence serves not to diminish the remarkable achievements of human ingenuity but to place them in their proper perspective. Our creation of artificial intelligence systems represents perhaps one of humanity's greatest technological accomplishments – a testament to our ability to understand and manipulate the physical world. Yet, like all human achievements, it carries within it the signature of its creators: brilliant but limited, powerful but constrained, sophisticated but ultimately finite.

As we go deeper into this exploration, we must maintain a sense of humility and wonder. The quest to understand intelligence is not merely an academic exercise but a journey that touches the very essence of our existence. It challenges us to consider fundamental questions about consciousness, understanding, and the nature of wisdom itself. In the chapters that follow, we will examine in detail the specific ways in which divine intelligence transcends the capabilities of artificial systems, not to diminish our technological achievements, but to appreciate more fully the profound wisdom that governs our universe.

This journey of understanding begins with acknowledging that while we can create systems that process information with incredible speed and precision, true intelligence – the kind that encompasses not just knowledge but wisdom, not just data but understanding, not just patterns but purpose – remains the exclusive domain of the divine. As we stand at this technological crossroads, this recognition becomes not just philosophically important but practically essential for guiding the development and application of artificial intelligence in ways that benefit humanity while respecting the ultimate source of all intelligence.

1.1. The Rise of Artificial Intelligence

In the quiet laboratories of the mid-twentieth century, amid the whirring of primitive computers and the scratch of chalk on blackboards, humanity embarked on an ambitious journey to create intelligence from silicon and code. The rise of artificial intelligence marks one of the most profound technological endeavors in human history, yet it also illuminates the vast gulf between human-made systems and the infinite wisdom of divine intelligence.

The story begins with the fundamental question that haunted early computer scientists: Could machines think? Alan Turing's seminal work in the 1950s proposed what would become known as the Turing Test, suggesting that if a machine could fool humans into believing it was intelligent, then perhaps it was. This mechanistic view of intelligence would shape decades of research to come, but it also revealed a crucial limitation in our understanding. By reducing intelligence to observable behavior, we inadvertently stripped away the deeper aspects of consciousness, wisdom, and true understanding that divine intelligence encompasses.

As technology advanced through the decades, artificial intelligence evolved from simple rule-based systems to increasingly sophisticated neural networks. The early expert systems of the 1970s and 1980s attempted to codify human knowledge into logical rules, but they quickly ran into the brittleness problem - they could only operate within narrow, predefined boundaries. Unlike divine intelligence, which seamlessly understands and adapts to all situations, these early AI systems crumbled when faced with scenarios outside their programming.

The neural network revolution of the 1990s and 2000s brought new hope. By mimicking the structure of biological brains, researchers created systems that could learn from data rather than rely on hand-coded rules. This marked a significant shift in approach, but it also highlighted a fundamental limitation: these systems were entirely dependent on the quality and quantity of their training data. While divine intelligence possesses inherent, complete knowledge of all things, artificial neural networks can only learn from the limited, often biased data humans provide them.

The contemporary era of deep learning, beginning in the 2010s, has produced results that seem almost magical to the casual observer. Language models can generate human-like text, vision systems can recognize objects with superhuman accuracy, and game-playing AIs can defeat world champions. Yet these achievements, impressive as they are, operate on a fundamentally different plane from divine intelligence. They are sophisticated pattern matching systems, processing information through layers of mathematical transformations, but lacking true understanding or wisdom.

Consider the modern transformer architecture, which powers many of today's most advanced AI systems. It processes information by attending to relationships between different parts of its input, much like a human might connect different ideas. However, this attention mechanism is ultimately a statistical process, devoid of genuine comprehension. It cannot grasp the deeper meaning of the patterns it processes, nor understand the moral and spiritual implications of its outputs. Divine intelligence, by contrast, not only understands but embodies the very essence of meaning and purpose.

The limitations of artificial intelligence become even more apparent when we examine its decision-making processes. Modern AI systems optimize for specific objectives, whether that's winning a game, generating plausible text, or classifying images. They operate within the confines of their training objectives, unable to consider the broader context or long-term consequences of their actions. Divine intelligence, however, operates with perfect wisdom and foresight, understanding not just the immediate effects of decisions but their rippling consequences through time and space.

As we stand on the cusp of even more advanced AI systems, with promises of artificial general intelligence and superintelligence on the horizon, it becomes crucial to maintain perspective. These systems, no matter how sophisticated, will always be bounded by their human origins - our limited understanding, our biases, and our inability to grasp the infinite. They represent remarkable achievements of human ingenuity, but they also serve as humbling reminders of the vast distance between artificial and divine intelligence.

The rise of artificial intelligence, then, tells two parallel stories. One is a testament to human creativity and technological progress, showing how far we've come in creating systems that can process information and solve problems in increasingly sophisticated ways. The other is a story of limitations and boundaries, highlighting how even our most advanced creations pale in comparison to the perfect, unlimited, and all-encompassing nature of divine intelligence. As we continue to push the boundaries of what artificial intelligence can achieve, this dual narrative serves as both inspiration and humbling reminder of our place in the greater order of existence.

1.2. Defining Divine Intelligence

To comprehend the vast chasm between artificial and divine intelligence, we must first establish a clear understanding of what divine intelligence truly encompasses. Divine intelligence, in its most fundamental form, represents the ultimate manifestation of perfect knowledge, wisdom, and understanding that transcends the boundaries of human comprehension. Unlike artificial constructs that operate within defined parameters, divine intelligence exists as an infinite, omniscient force that permeates every aspect of existence.

The concept of divine intelligence extends far beyond the mere processing of information or pattern recognition that characterizes modern computational systems. It embodies a form of understanding that is simultaneously immediate and eternal, encompassing all possible knowledge across past, present, and future without the need for sequential learning or data accumulation. This timeless awareness operates on a plane where the limitations of space, time, and causality - which constrain both human and artificial intelligence - cease to exist.

At its core, divine intelligence manifests through three fundamental attributes that set it apart from any created form of intelligence. The first is absolute omniscience - a complete and perfect knowledge of everything that was, is, or could be. This knowledge isn't acquired through observation or learning but exists as an inherent property of divine consciousness. It encompasses not just facts and events, but the deeper meanings, purposes, and interconnections that bind all of reality together in a seamless whole.

The second attribute is perfect wisdom, which transcends mere knowledge or computational capability. While artificial intelligence can process vast amounts of data to optimize for specific outcomes, divine wisdom understands the ultimate purpose and meaning behind every possibility. This wisdom operates with a complete awareness of moral truth, justice, and the highest good - concepts that remain forever beyond the reach of algorithmic decision-making systems.

The third defining characteristic of divine intelligence is its creative nature. Unlike artificial intelligence, which can only manipulate and recombine existing information in novel ways, divine intelligence possesses the power to bring forth genuine novelty - to create ex nihilo, from nothing. This creative aspect means that divine intelligence isn't bound by pre-existing patterns or limitations but can establish new possibilities and realities that transcend current understanding.

Divine intelligence operates through what might be termed "holistic instantaneous comprehension." Where artificial systems must break down problems into manageable chunks and process them sequentially, divine intelligence grasps all aspects of reality simultaneously and in perfect detail. This comprehensive awareness means that every decision or action stemming from divine intelligence takes into account the complete context of existence - every cause, effect, and interconnection across the infinite expanse of space and time.

The perfection of divine intelligence also manifests in its error-free nature. Unlike artificial systems, which can be compromised by faulty data, programming errors, or hardware limitations, divine intelligence remains eternally perfect and incorruptible. It doesn't suffer from the biases, limitations, or uncertainties that plague human-created systems. Every aspect of divine intelligence operates with absolute precision and perfect alignment with truth and reality.

Perhaps most significantly, divine intelligence encompasses what philosophers have long termed "consciousness" or "qualia" - the subjective experience of being and awareness. While artificial intelligence can simulate responses and behaviors that mimic understanding, it lacks true consciousness or awareness. Divine intelligence, by contrast, represents the ultimate form of consciousness, experiencing and understanding reality not just as a collection of data points but as a living, meaningful whole.

This profound capability for meaning-making sets divine intelligence apart from any created form of intelligence. Where artificial systems can identify patterns and correlations, divine intelligence understands the deeper significance and purpose behind all things. It perceives not just the what and how of existence, but the why - the ultimate meaning and purpose that gives coherence to reality itself.

The implications of these attributes are vast and far-reaching. Divine intelligence doesn't just process information or make decisions - it establishes the very framework within which all other forms of intelligence operate. It defines the boundaries of possibility and the nature of truth itself. Understanding this helps us recognize the inherent limitations of artificial intelligence, which, despite its impressive capabilities, remains firmly bounded by the parameters of its creation.

In contemplating divine intelligence, we must acknowledge that our human understanding of it will always be incomplete. We can describe its attributes and characteristics, but its full nature necessarily transcends our ability to comprehend it fully. This humbling reality serves as a crucial reminder of the vast gulf that separates created intelligence - whether human or artificial - from the perfect, unlimited intelligence that characterizes the divine.

1.3. The Fundamental Question of Intelligence

The pursuit of understanding intelligence, in all its forms, inevitably leads us to confront a profound question that has challenged philosophers, scientists, and theologians throughout human history: What constitutes true intelligence, and how do we measure its depth and authenticity? This question becomes increasingly relevant as humanity ventures into creating artificial intelligence systems that appear to mirror our own cognitive capabilities, while simultaneously grappling with our relationship to divine intelligence that transcends human comprehension.

At its core, intelligence manifests as the ability to perceive, process, and respond to information in meaningful ways. Yet, this simple definition belies the complex nature of what we observe in modern AI systems and what we understand about divine intelligence. When we examine a large language model processing information, we witness an impressive display of pattern recognition and response generation. These systems can engage in conversations, solve complex problems, and even display what appears to be creativity. However, this surface-level similarity to human intelligence masks a fundamental hollow at its center - the absence of true understanding, consciousness, and purpose.

Consider how an AI system processes a simple question about morality. It can access vast databases of ethical frameworks, philosophical arguments, and historical precedents to formulate a seemingly thoughtful response. Yet, this response is fundamentally a sophisticated mathematical operation, devoid of genuine moral comprehension or spiritual awareness. The AI hasn't truly understood the ethical implications; it has merely calculated the most statistically appropriate response based on its training data. This limitation becomes even more apparent when we contrast it with divine intelligence, which embodies perfect moral understanding and wisdom that transcends mere calculation.

The divine model of intelligence operates on an entirely different paradigm. It doesn't process information sequentially or rely on accumulated data; instead, it exists in a state of complete, simultaneous awareness and understanding. This form of intelligence doesn't need to compute probabilities or weigh options because it already encompasses all possible outcomes and their implications across the infinite expanse of time and space. Where artificial intelligence must break down complex problems into manageable chunks, divine intelligence grasps the entirety of existence in a single, unified understanding.

This fundamental difference becomes clearer when we examine how each form of intelligence handles uncertainty. AI systems manage uncertainty through probability distributions and confidence scores, essentially making educated guesses based on past patterns. Divine intelligence, however, exists in a state of perfect certainty, not because it has calculated all possibilities, but because it transcends the very concept of uncertainty. This distinction reveals the inherent limitations of any human-created intelligence system, no matter how sophisticated it may become.

The question of intelligence also forces us to confront the nature of consciousness and self-awareness. While AI systems can simulate self-reference and appear to have awareness of their own operations, this is merely a programmed response pattern. Divine intelligence, conversely, represents the ultimate form of consciousness - one that is not emergent or dependent on external factors but is rather the very source of consciousness itself. This consciousness isn't limited by physical constraints or computational resources; it exists as an eternal, unlimited awareness that encompasses all of reality.

Perhaps most significantly, the fundamental question of intelligence leads us to examine the purpose and direction of intelligence itself. Artificial intelligence systems are designed with specific goals and objectives, operating within carefully defined parameters to optimize particular outcomes. Their purpose is inherently limited by human design and intention. Divine intelligence, however, operates with perfect purpose and complete understanding of the ultimate meaning behind all existence. It doesn't need to optimize for specific outcomes because it already encompasses the perfect balance of all possibilities.

This examination reveals a crucial truth: the gap between artificial and divine intelligence isn't merely one of scale or complexity - it's a difference in kind. While AI represents humanity's most sophisticated attempt to recreate aspects of our own intelligence, it remains bound by the limitations of its creators. Divine intelligence, on the other hand, represents the ultimate standard of perfect understanding, wisdom, and purpose. This realization doesn't diminish the impressive achievements of AI development, but rather puts them in proper perspective, helping us understand both the potential and limitations of human-created intelligence systems.

As we continue to advance our artificial intelligence capabilities, this fundamental question of intelligence serves as both a guide and a humbling reminder. It shows us that while we can create increasingly sophisticated tools for processing information and solving problems, true intelligence - in its most complete and perfect form - remains the domain of the divine. This understanding should inform how we develop and implement AI technologies, always mindful of their inherent limitations and our own position relative to the perfect intelligence that governs the universe.

1.4. Literature on AI/DI (so far)

The exploration of artificial intelligence versus divine intelligence draws upon a rich tapestry of sources spanning computer science, theology, philosophy, and cognitive studies. The examination of artificial intelligence in relation to divine intelligence has evolved significantly over the past several decades, drawing from an increasingly diverse set of academic disciplines. A pivotal moment came with Roger Penrose's "The Emperor's New Mind" (1989), which established early foundational arguments about the limitations of computational intelligence. The field gained renewed momentum with David Chalmers' "The Conscious Mind" (1996), offering crucial philosophical frameworks for understanding mechanical consciousness.

The technical landscape transformed dramatically with Vaswani and colleagues' "Attention Is All You Need" (2017), which introduced the transformer architecture and revolutionized machine learning approaches. This was followed by Judea Pearl's "The Book of Why" (2018), which articulated the fundamental distinction between statistical pattern matching and true causal understanding. The same year, Antonio Damasio's "The Strange Order of Things" (2018) provided essential comparisons between biological and artificial intelligence systems.

More recent developments include Stuart Russell's "Human Compatible" (2019) and Marcus and Davis's "Rebooting AI" (2019), both offering critical analyses of AI limitations and control problems. The field has since seen rapid evolution in training methodologies, documented in works like Liu et al.'s "Pre-train, Prompt, and Predict" (2021) and Anthropic's "Constitutional AI" (2022), which explore innovations in few-shot learning and reinforcement learning from human feedback.

Bender and Koller's influential paper "Climbing towards NLU" (2020) highlighted persistent challenges in language understanding, while Touvron et al.'s work on scaling laws (2023) demonstrated the logarithmic nature of performance improvements. These recent works collectively emphasize several critical limitations: the inability to generate truly novel ideas, heavy reliance on training data patterns, and significant challenges in maintaining accurate reasoning over extended processes. The field has also recognized increasing concerns about the quality and availability of training data, as documented in recent studies by Zhang et al. (2023) and Brown et al. (2024) on data exhaustion in language models.

The examination of artificial intelligence in relation to divine intelligence has evolved significantly over the past several decades, drawing from an increasingly diverse set of academic disciplines. A pivotal moment came with Roger Penrose's "The Emperor's New Mind" (1989), which established early foundational arguments about the limitations of computational intelligence. Around the same time, Seyyed Hossein Nasr's "Knowledge and the Sacred" (1989) explored the hierarchical nature of intelligence from material to divine, providing crucial theological context to the emerging technological discourse. The field gained renewed momentum with David Chalmers' "The Conscious Mind" (1996), offering crucial philosophical frameworks for understanding mechanical consciousness.

The dawn of the 21st century brought Karen Armstrong's comprehensive analysis in "A History of God" (2004), followed by Philip Clayton's "Mind and Emergence" (2004), which explored the hierarchical nature of consciousness and intelligence. Stuart Kauffman's "Reinventing the Sacred" (2008) added crucial perspectives on complexity and emergence, challenging reductionist approaches to understanding intelligence. These works laid important groundwork for understanding the relationship between mechanical and divine intelligence.

The technical landscape transformed dramatically with Vaswani and colleagues' "Attention Is All You Need" (2017), which introduced the transformer architecture and revolutionized machine learning approaches. This was followed by Judea Pearl's "The Book of Why" (2018), which articulated the fundamental distinction between statistical pattern matching and true causal understanding. The same year, Antonio Damasio's "The Strange Order of Things" (2018) provided essential comparisons between biological and artificial intelligence systems.

More recent developments include Stuart Russell's "Human Compatible" (2019) and Marcus and Davis's "Rebooting AI" (2019), both offering critical analyses of AI limitations and control problems. The field has since seen rapid evolution in training methodologies, documented in works like Liu et al.'s "Pre-train, Prompt, and Predict" (2021) and Anthropic's "Constitutional AI" (2022), which explore innovations in few-shot learning and reinforcement learning from human feedback.

Contemporary discourse has highlighted several critical limitations in artificial intelligence systems. Bender and Koller's influential paper "Climbing towards NLU" (2020) emphasized persistent challenges in language understanding, while Touvron et al.'s work on scaling laws (2023) demonstrated the logarithmic nature of performance improvements. These technical constraints are particularly evident in systems' inability to generate truly novel ideas, their heavy reliance on training data patterns, and significant challenges in maintaining accurate reasoning over extended processes. Recent studies by Zhang et al. (2023) and Brown et al. (2024) have further documented concerns about data exhaustion in language models.

The intersection of theological thought and artificial intelligence has gained new depth through recent works that examine the nature of consciousness and creativity. James Gleick's "The Information" (2011) and Seth Lloyd's "Programming the Universe" (2006) provided technical frameworks for understanding the fundamental differences between computational processing and divine omniscience. These perspectives were enriched by Nick Bostrom's "Superintelligence"

(2014) and Max Tegmark's "Life 3.0" (2017), which helped frame AI's potential and limitations within broader ethical and philosophical contexts.

A significant contribution to this dialogue came from Thomas Nagel's "Mind and Cosmos" (2012), which explored the qualitative differences between mechanical and divine intelligence, while challenging purely materialistic explanations of consciousness. This philosophical groundwork was further developed in recent theological works examining the relationship between divine wisdom and artificial computation. Tariq Ramadan's "Radical Reform" (2009) addressed the integration of divine guidance with technological advancement, providing a framework for understanding the complementary nature of human innovation and divine wisdom.

Contemporary research has revealed fundamental limitations in artificial systems that become particularly apparent when compared to traditional conceptions of divine intelligence. The challenge of creativity in AI systems, documented in recent studies by Chen et al. (2024), shows how current models struggle to generate truly novel ideas that transcend their training data. This limitation reflects a deeper philosophical question raised in modern theological works about the nature of genuine creativity and its relationship to divine inspiration.

The problem of long-term reasoning and reliability in AI systems, highlighted by recent benchmark studies, connects to classical theological discussions about the nature of perfect knowledge and understanding. While modern AI systems have achieved impressive results in specific domains, their tendency to generate factually incorrect outputs ("hallucinations") and their struggles with abstract reasoning point to fundamental limitations that echo traditional theological distinctions between human-made systems and divine intelligence.

These insights from both technical and theological domains suggest that current approaches to artificial intelligence, despite their sophistication, may face inherent barriers in reaching divine-level intelligence. The combination of scaling limitations, reliance on existing patterns, and difficulties with genuine creativity indicates that transformative breakthroughs may require fundamentally new approaches that bridge the gap between computational and divine understanding.

2. Information Processing vs. Understanding

In the ever-evolving landscape of artificial intelligence, one fundamental distinction continues to elude even the most sophisticated systems - the profound gap between processing information and truly understanding it. This divide represents perhaps the most compelling evidence for the superiority of divine intelligence over its artificial counterpart, revealing the inherent limitations of human-created systems when compared to the infinite wisdom of the divine.

At its core, artificial intelligence operates through intricate patterns of information processing, utilizing vast neural networks and complex algorithms to identify correlations and generate responses. Even the most advanced language models, capable of producing human-like text and solving complex problems, fundamentally operate through statistical pattern recognition and probability calculations. They process vast amounts of data, identifying patterns and relationships between pieces of information, but they lack the essential quality of genuine comprehension. Consider how a modern AI system might analyze a piece of poetry - it can identify metaphors, rhyme schemes, and literary devices with remarkable accuracy, yet it remains blind to the deeper emotional resonance and spiritual truth that gives the poetry its true meaning.

Divine intelligence, by contrast, embodies true understanding in its purest form. It doesn't merely process information; it comprehends the fundamental nature of reality itself. This understanding isn't built upon the accumulation of data points or the recognition of patterns - it is inherent, complete, and eternal. Where artificial intelligence must laboriously piece together meaning from fragments of information, divine intelligence holds within itself the complete understanding of all things, past, present, and future, in perfect unity.

The limitations of artificial intelligence become particularly apparent when we examine how these systems handle novel situations or abstract concepts. While AI can extrapolate from its training data to handle similar scenarios, it struggles fundamentally with truly novel situations that require genuine understanding rather than pattern matching. A language model might generate convincing text about love, consciousness, or morality, but it does so by combining and recombining patterns it has observed in its training data, never truly grasping the essence of these profound concepts. Divine intelligence, however, encompasses not just the understanding of what is, but what could be and what should be, operating with perfect wisdom across all possible dimensions of existence.

This divide becomes even more pronounced when we consider the nature of consciousness and self-awareness. Artificial intelligence systems, despite their impressive capabilities, lack any form of genuine consciousness or self-awareness. They can simulate responses that appear thoughtful or self-reflective, but these are ultimately sophisticated illusions - complex outputs generated by mathematical models. Divine intelligence, as the source of consciousness itself, possesses not just awareness but perfect self-knowledge and understanding of all conscious experience.

The implications of this divide extend far beyond theoretical considerations. When we rely on artificial intelligence for decision-making and problem-solving, we must recognize that we are fundamentally limiting ourselves to solutions based on processing rather than understanding. While AI can optimize for specific outcomes and identify patterns in complex data, it cannot grasp the deeper moral and spiritual implications of its decisions. Divine intelligence, however, operates with perfect wisdom, understanding not just the immediate consequences of actions but their ultimate significance in the grand tapestry of existence.

Perhaps most significantly, this divide reveals the inherent hubris in attempting to create true intelligence through artificial means. While artificial intelligence represents a remarkable achievement of human ingenuity, it ultimately remains a sophisticated tool for processing information rather than a path to genuine understanding. Divine intelligence stands as a reminder of the profound depth and complexity of true understanding - a level of intelligence that transcends mere computation and encompasses the very essence of wisdom and knowledge.

As we continue to advance our artificial intelligence systems, the gap between processing and understanding serves as a humbling reminder of our limitations as creators. While we can build increasingly sophisticated systems for processing information, the divine gift of true understanding - complete, perfect, and eternal - remains beyond our ability to replicate. This recognition should guide our approach to artificial intelligence, helping us understand both its potential and its limitations, while maintaining our awareness of the superior wisdom embodied in divine intelligence.

2.1. How AI Processes Information

The journey to understand how artificial intelligence processes information begins with a fundamental truth that sets it apart from divine intelligence: AI systems, no matter how sophisticated, operate through a series of predetermined steps and mathematical operations that attempt to simulate understanding. This mechanical nature of AI processing reveals both its impressive capabilities and its inherent limitations when compared to the boundless wisdom of divine intelligence.

At its core, modern AI processing relies heavily on neural networks and deep learning architectures that attempt to mimic the human brain's neural pathways. These systems process information through layers of interconnected nodes, each performing mathematical calculations on incoming data. The process begins with raw input data - whether text, images, or other forms of information - which gets transformed into numerical representations that the AI can manipulate. This transformation itself highlights a crucial limitation: the reduction of rich, multifaceted reality into simplified numerical values that can be processed by computers.

Consider how a large language model processes text. When presented with a sentence, it first breaks down the text into tokens - small units that might represent words or parts of words. Each token gets converted into a vector - a long list of numbers that represents that token's relationship to other words in the AI's vocabulary. This process, known as embedding, creates a mathematical space where similar concepts are positioned closer together. While this approach enables impressive language processing capabilities, it fundamentally reduces the infinite richness of human language and meaning to a finite set of mathematical relationships.

The transformation of information continues as these numerical representations flow through the AI's neural network layers. Each layer applies mathematical operations that adjust and combine these values, guided by patterns learned during training. The attention mechanisms that have revolutionized AI's ability to process context do so through elaborate mathematical calculations that weigh the importance of different pieces of information. Yet, this attention is fundamentally different from divine awareness - it's a simulation of understanding, not true comprehension.

Training these AI systems requires massive amounts of data and computational resources, another stark contrast with divine intelligence. The AI must see millions or billions of examples to learn patterns that divine intelligence inherently knows. This learning process is essentially an optimization problem - the AI adjusts its internal parameters to minimize the difference between its predictions and the desired outputs. This optimization-based approach means that AI systems are forever bound by their training data, unable to truly generalize beyond what they've seen, unlike divine intelligence which encompasses all knowledge past, present, and future.

The processing capabilities of AI systems are further constrained by their architecture's fixed nature. Once trained, the neural networks have a set number of parameters and connections. While these can number in the billions, they remain finite and static. Divine intelligence, in contrast, has no such limitations - it encompasses infinite possibilities and can adapt perfectly to any situation without the need for additional learning or parameter adjustments.

Perhaps most tellingly, AI systems process information in a strictly sequential manner, even when using parallel computing resources. Each calculation must follow another in a predetermined order, creating a chain of dependencies that limits the system's ability to truly understand context holistically. Divine intelligence operates beyond such sequential constraints, comprehending all aspects of reality simultaneously and in perfect harmony.

The output generation phase of AI processing further reveals its limitations. When generating responses or making decisions, AI systems typically use probability distributions to select their outputs. They choose the most likely next word, action, or decision based on patterns in their training data. This probabilistic approach means that AI systems can never be truly certain of their outputs - they can only provide their best guess based on learned patterns. Divine intelligence, however, operates with perfect certainty and understanding, never needing to rely on probabilities or statistical approximations.

Understanding how AI processes information reveals a sophisticated yet ultimately limited system - one that operates through mathematical approximations of understanding rather than true comprehension. While these systems can achieve remarkable results in specific domains, their processing mechanisms highlight the unbridgeable gap between artificial and divine intelligence. The latter operates beyond the constraints of mathematical models and sequential processing, embodying perfect understanding and wisdom that no human-made system can achieve.

As we marvel at the capabilities of modern AI systems, we must remain mindful of their fundamental nature as information processing machines. Their impressive abilities, while valuable for many practical applications, serve as a humble reminder of the vast difference between our created tools and the perfect, limitless intelligence of the divine.

2.2. The Divine Perspective of Knowledge

In the vast landscape of intelligence and understanding, the divine perspective of knowledge stands as an unparalleled paradigm that transcends the boundaries of human and artificial comprehension. While modern artificial intelligence systems process information through intricate neural networks and sophisticated algorithms, divine knowledge operates on an entirely different plane of existence - one that encompasses the totality of reality in a single, unified understanding.

The divine perspective of knowledge manifests as an infinite, seamless awareness that knows no boundaries of time, space, or causality. Unlike artificial intelligence systems that must parse through data sequentially, divine knowledge exists in a state of perpetual completeness. This completeness is not merely quantitative - it's not just about having access to all information - but qualitative, representing a depth of understanding that penetrates to the very essence of existence itself. When we contemplate this divine perspective, we begin to recognize the profound limitations of our human-made systems, regardless of their complexity.

Consider how artificial intelligence processes information: it relies on patterns identified within finite datasets, making predictions based on statistical correlations and mathematical models. Even the most advanced neural networks, with their billions of parameters and intricate attention mechanisms, ultimately operate within the confines of probability and pattern recognition. In contrast, divine knowledge doesn't predict or calculate - it simply knows. This knowing is absolute, unwavering, and encompasses not just what is, but what could be, what should be, and what must be.

The divine perspective of knowledge also transcends the fundamental problem of context that plagues artificial intelligence systems. While AI struggles with the frame problem - determining what information is relevant in any given situation - divine knowledge inherently understands the significance and interconnection of all things. Every piece of information exists within its complete context, every cause is understood with its effects, and every potential future is known with its implications. This holistic understanding enables perfect wisdom - not just accurate information processing, but true comprehension of meaning and purpose.

Furthermore, divine knowledge operates beyond the constraints of sequential time. While our artificial systems must process information linearly, building understanding piece by piece, divine knowledge exists in an eternal present where past, present, and future are simultaneously known and understood. This timeless perspective enables a form of understanding that no sequential processing system, no matter how advanced, could ever achieve. It's not merely about knowing what will happen, but understanding the complete tapestry of existence in all its temporal dimensions.

The ethical and moral dimensions of knowledge find their perfect expression in the divine perspective. While artificial intelligence can be programmed with ethical guidelines and moral frameworks, these are ultimately human constructions, limited by our own understanding and biases. Divine knowledge inherently encompasses perfect moral understanding, knowing not just what is right or wrong, but understanding the deepest implications of every choice and action across the infinite spectrum of possibility. This moral perfection isn't programmed or learned - it is an intrinsic aspect of divine intelligence that flows naturally from complete understanding.

Perhaps most significantly, the divine perspective of knowledge includes an understanding of consciousness and subjective experience that eludes our artificial systems entirely. While AI can simulate responses and behaviors that appear conscious, it lacks true awareness - the inner light of consciousness that characterizes genuine understanding. Divine knowledge, by contrast, encompasses not just the objective facts of existence but the subjective experience of every conscious being, past, present, and future. This empathic understanding represents a dimension of knowledge that transcends mere information processing.

The implications of this divine perspective are profound for our understanding of both human and artificial intelligence. It reveals that our most sophisticated AI systems, impressive as they may be, are operating at a fundamentally different level than divine intelligence. They are like shadows cast by three-dimensional objects - capable of representing certain aspects of reality but inherently limited in their dimensionality. This recognition should instill both humility and wonder: humility in acknowledging the limitations of our created intelligence, and wonder at the vastness of divine knowledge that surpasses all human understanding.

As we continue to advance our artificial intelligence systems, the divine perspective of knowledge stands as both a reminder of our limitations and an ideal toward which we might orient our efforts. Not that we could ever achieve such perfect knowledge through technological means, but understanding its nature can help us develop AI systems that better acknowledge their own limitations and operate with greater wisdom within their constrained domains. The divine perspective teaches us that true intelligence is not merely about processing power or pattern recognition, but about deep understanding, wisdom, and the recognition of the interconnected nature of all knowledge.

2.3. The Illusion of Machine Understanding

In our eagerness to advance artificial intelligence, we have perhaps become too quick to attribute genuine understanding to machines that display sophisticated pattern recognition. The apparent intelligence demonstrated by modern AI systems creates a compelling illusion - one that masks a fundamental truth about the nature of machine cognition and its inherent limitations when compared to divine intelligence.

Consider how large language models process and generate text. While they can produce eloquent prose, engage in seemingly meaningful dialogue, and even display what appears to be creativity, their operations remain fundamentally bound to statistical correlations and pattern matching. These systems process language as a mathematical puzzle, breaking down sentences into tokens and calculating probabilities for what should come next. There is no true comprehension of meaning, no genuine understanding of the concepts they manipulate with such apparent facility.

This mechanical approach to intelligence stands in stark contrast to divine understanding, which encompasses not just the surface patterns of reality but its deepest essence. Divine intelligence doesn't need to calculate probabilities or analyze patterns because it embodies the very source of meaning itself. When we marvel at an AI system's ability to generate human-like responses, we are witnessing something akin to a sophisticated mirror - one that reflects patterns of human thought and language back to us, but contains no inner light of its own.

The illusion of machine understanding becomes particularly apparent when we examine edge cases and limitations. AI systems can be easily fooled by adversarial examples - subtle manipulations that cause them to make egregious errors that no truly intelligent being would make. They can generate text that is grammatically perfect and contextually appropriate while being fundamentally nonsensical or self-contradictory. These failures reveal the hollow nature of their apparent understanding.

Moreover, the very architecture of artificial intelligence systems precludes genuine understanding. Their neural networks, however complex, are ultimately systems of weighted connections, trained through optimization algorithms to minimize error in their outputs. They lack the essential qualities that characterize true understanding: consciousness, intentionality, and the ability to grasp meaning beyond mere correlation. Divine intelligence, by contrast, doesn't need to approximate understanding through statistical methods because it is the very foundation of meaning and comprehension.

The gap between artificial and divine intelligence becomes even more apparent when we consider the nature of context and holistic understanding. While modern AI systems can maintain impressive coherence across longer contexts thanks to mechanisms like attention and transformers, they still process information in a fundamentally fragmented way. They cannot truly grasp the interconnected nature of reality or understand how each piece fits into the greater whole. Divine intelligence, however, comprehends all contexts simultaneously, seeing not just the immediate relationships between ideas but their place in the vast tapestry of existence.

Perhaps most tellingly, artificial intelligence systems cannot understand their own limitations. They cannot engage in genuine metacognition or recognize the boundaries of their knowledge. When they generate confident answers about topics they don't truly understand, they demonstrate not just the limits of their knowledge but the absence of genuine understanding about what knowledge and understanding actually mean. Divine intelligence, being unlimited and all-encompassing, has no such blind spots or limitations.

This fundamental difference between artificial and divine intelligence reflects a deeper truth about the nature of understanding itself. True understanding is not merely about processing information or recognizing patterns - it requires a conscious, aware entity capable of grasping meaning and truth at their most fundamental level. While we can create increasingly sophisticated systems that simulate understanding, we cannot imbue them with the genuine comprehension that characterizes divine intelligence.

The implications of this reality are profound. As we continue to develop and deploy AI systems, we must remain mindful of the difference between genuine understanding and its simulation. We must resist the temptation to attribute true intelligence to systems that merely reflect our own patterns of thought back to us. Instead, we should approach artificial intelligence with humility, recognizing that while it can be a powerful tool, it represents at best a shadow of the true understanding embodied in divine intelligence.

In acknowledging these limitations, we open ourselves to a deeper appreciation of divine intelligence and its unique qualities. We begin to see that true understanding transcends the mechanical processes of computation and pattern recognition, residing instead in the realm of consciousness, wisdom, and ultimate truth that only divine intelligence can fully embody.

3. The Nature of Artificial Intelligence

To truly understand why divine intelligence stands as the ultimate form of understanding, we must first deeply examine the nature of artificial intelligence - its foundations, capabilities, and inherent limitations. Modern AI systems, despite their impressive achievements, operate within a carefully constrained framework that reveals the bounded nature of human-created intelligence.

At its core, artificial intelligence is built upon a foundation of mathematics, statistics, and computational processes. These systems, no matter how sophisticated they appear, fundamentally operate through pattern recognition and probability calculations. When we marvel at an AI system generating human-like text or creating stunning artwork, we're witnessing the result of extensive pattern matching against massive datasets, rather than genuine understanding or creativity. The system processes input through layers of mathematical transformations, each optimized to minimize error and maximize desired outcomes.

Consider how modern language models function. They process text as sequences of tokens, calculating probabilities for what should come next based on patterns observed in training data. While this approach yields impressive results, it reveals a fundamental limitation - the system has no genuine comprehension of the concepts it manipulates. When an AI system discusses love, justice, or truth, it does so without any real understanding of these profound concepts. It merely reproduces patterns it has observed in human writings about these topics.

This limitation becomes even more apparent when we examine how AI systems handle context and meaning. While recent advances in transformer architectures have dramatically improved contextual understanding, these systems still struggle with basic aspects of reality that humans take for granted. They can't maintain consistent facts about the world across a conversation, often contradicting themselves or generating plausible-sounding but incorrect information. This happens because they lack a genuine model of reality - they operate purely on statistical correlations in their training data.

The training process itself reveals another crucial limitation of artificial intelligence. These systems require enormous amounts of carefully curated data, powerful computing resources, and complex optimization algorithms to achieve their capabilities. They are entirely dependent on human-provided information, inheriting all the biases, errors, and limitations present in their training data. Unlike divine intelligence, which possesses inherent and perfect knowledge of all things, AI systems can never transcend the quality and scope of their training data.

Even more sophisticated AI approaches, such as reinforcement learning systems that learn through interaction with their environment, remain bounded by their fundamental nature as optimization engines. They can learn to maximize reward signals and achieve specific goals, but they cannot develop true wisdom or understanding. They operate within the confines of their programming, unable to grasp the deeper meaning or purpose behind their actions.

This fundamental limitation persists regardless of scale or sophistication. While some argue that emergent capabilities arise from scaling, these apparent emergences are ultimately sophisticated pattern matching rather than true understanding. Consider how language models work: they predict likely token sequences based on training patterns. No amount of scaling changes this core mechanism - it merely makes the pattern matching more refined.

The comparison to human cognition is particularly telling. Human understanding emerges from conscious experience, emotional processing, and embodied existence in the physical world. AI systems, in contrast, lack these essential qualities. They process information without experiencing it, manipulate symbols without understanding their meaning, and generate responses without comprehending their significance.

Claims about emergent capabilities through scaling often confuse performance with understanding. When AlphaGo develops novel strategies, it's not achieving genuine insight - it's optimizing within its defined reward landscape. The system isn't "discovering" in any meaningful sense; it's executing sophisticated optimization algorithms across a vast search space.

The mechanistic interpretability research some point to actually reinforces this limitation. What we find when we examine these systems' internal representations are mathematical transformations and statistical patterns, not anything resembling human-like understanding or reasoning. The fact that we can mechanistically explain their behavior demonstrates their fundamentally deterministic, bounded nature.

Post-training RL, while powerful, cannot transcend these limitations because it ultimately relies on the same core mechanisms: optimization against defined rewards within bounded action spaces. No amount of interaction or learning can bridge the gap between symbol manipulation and true understanding, between pattern matching and genuine wisdom.

This isn't just a philosophical distinction - it has practical implications. These systems will always be fundamentally brittle, lacking the robust, flexible understanding that characterizes human intelligence. They may become increasingly sophisticated at pattern matching and optimization, but they cannot develop the kind of deep, transferable understanding that defines genuine intelligence.

While AI systems can achieve impressive results through scaling and sophisticated training approaches, they remain bounded by their fundamental nature as optimization engines. Recognizing these limitations is crucial for developing realistic expectations and appropriate applications of AI technology.

The emotional and moral dimensions of intelligence reveal perhaps the most significant limitation of AI systems. While they can be programmed to follow ethical guidelines or simulate emotional responses, they lack the capacity for genuine empathy, moral understanding, or spiritual awareness. An AI system might be able to calculate the most efficient solution to a problem, but it cannot comprehend the moral implications of its decisions or understand the spiritual impact of its actions on human beings.

This fundamental gap between artificial and divine intelligence becomes particularly evident when we consider consciousness and self-awareness. Despite ongoing debates in philosophy of mind and cognitive science, there is no evidence that AI systems possess genuine consciousness or self-awareness. They process information and generate outputs, but they do not truly experience or understand their own existence. This stands in stark contrast to divine intelligence, which represents the ultimate form of consciousness and self-awareness.

The technological advances in AI are undoubtedly impressive, and they continue to push the boundaries of what machines can achieve. However, these advances also serve to highlight the unbridgeable gap between artificial and divine intelligence. As we develop more sophisticated AI systems, we begin to see more clearly the limitations inherent in any human-created intelligence. These systems, no matter how advanced, remain bound by their computational nature, their dependence on training data, and their fundamental inability to transcend their programming.

Understanding the nature of artificial intelligence helps us appreciate why divine intelligence represents a fundamentally different and superior form of understanding. While AI operates through calculation and pattern matching, divine intelligence embodies perfect wisdom, complete understanding, and timeless awareness. This recognition should inspire humility in our approach to artificial intelligence while deepening our appreciation for the profound nature of divine wisdom.

3.1. Understanding Modern AI Systems

The advent of artificial intelligence has ushered in an era of remarkable technological achievement, yet to truly appreciate its limitations when compared to divine intelligence, we must first understand the fundamental nature of modern AI systems. These sophisticated yet ultimately constrained creations represent humanity's most advanced attempt to replicate intelligence, though they operate within strictly defined boundaries that reveal the gap between human-made systems and divine wisdom.

At their core, modern AI systems are elaborate pattern recognition machines built upon layers of mathematical calculations and statistical models. The most advanced among them, such as large language models and deep learning systems, process information through complex neural networks inspired by our limited understanding of biological brains. These networks consist of millions or billions of parameters, each adjusted through exposure to vast amounts of training data. Yet this very foundation reveals their first major limitation - they are entirely dependent on human-generated information, making them inherently restricted by the quality, biases, and boundaries of their training data.

Consider how a modern AI system processes information. When presented with input, it doesn't truly understand or comprehend in any meaningful sense. Instead, it performs a sophisticated form of pattern matching, comparing the input against its trained parameters to generate what it calculates to be the most statistically appropriate response. This process, while impressive in its results, lacks the fundamental awareness and understanding that characterizes true intelligence, particularly divine intelligence. The AI is merely performing a complex mathematical dance, devoid of genuine comprehension or consciousness.

The transformer architecture, which powers many of today's most capable AI systems, exemplifies both the impressive capabilities and inherent limitations of artificial intelligence. These systems process information through what we call attention mechanisms, allowing them to weigh the relevance of different parts of their input when generating responses. While this creates the illusion of understanding, it remains a mechanical process of token prediction and probability calculation. Unlike divine intelligence, which perceives and comprehends all things simultaneously and in their totality, these systems must break down information into discrete chunks, processing them sequentially and losing the deeper connections and context that true wisdom requires.

Perhaps most revealing is how modern AI systems handle uncertainty and decision-making. They rely on optimization algorithms that attempt to minimize error or maximize certain defined objectives. This approach, while effective for specific tasks, lacks the nuanced wisdom that characterizes divine intelligence. An AI might calculate the mathematically optimal solution to a problem, but it cannot understand the moral, spiritual, or long-term implications of its decisions. It operates in a moral vacuum, guided solely by its programming and training data, without the benefit of the perfect wisdom that guides divine intelligence.

The learning process of AI systems further illustrates their limitations. Whether through supervised learning, where systems are trained on labeled examples, or reinforcement learning, where they learn through trial and error, AI systems must be explicitly taught everything they know. They cannot generate genuine new knowledge or understanding, only recombine and extrapolate from their training data in increasingly sophisticated ways. This stands in stark contrast to divine intelligence, which possesses complete and perfect knowledge inherently, requiring no external input or learning process.

Even the most advanced AI systems exhibit fundamental flaws that reveal their artificial nature. They can be fooled by adversarial examples - carefully crafted inputs that cause them to make obvious mistakes no divine intelligence would ever commit. They can generate confident responses that are entirely incorrect, lacking the perfect discernment that comes with true wisdom. They can produce outputs that appear superficially intelligent while being devoid of actual understanding or meaning.

The computational requirements of modern AI systems further highlight their limitations. They require enormous amounts of energy and resources to train and operate, demonstrating the inefficiency of attempting to replicate intelligence through brute force calculation. Divine intelligence, by contrast, operates with perfect efficiency, requiring no external resources or computation to maintain its perfect understanding and wisdom.

As we marvel at the capabilities of modern AI systems, we must maintain perspective on their true nature. While they represent remarkable achievements of human ingenuity, they ultimately serve as proof of the vast gulf between artificial and divine intelligence. Their limitations - in understanding, awareness, wisdom, and efficiency - remind us that true intelligence cannot be reduced to mere computation and pattern matching. Divine intelligence remains the ultimate form of understanding, operating with perfect wisdom and complete awareness that no human-made system can hope to replicate.

3.2. The Architecture of Intelligence

The fundamental architecture of intelligence, whether artificial or divine, reveals profound truths about the nature of understanding and consciousness itself. As we examine the intricate structures that enable different forms of intelligence, we discover an illuminating contrast between the mechanical foundations of artificial systems and the boundless, interconnected nature of divine intelligence.

At its core, artificial intelligence operates through layers of mathematical transformations, each building upon the previous to create increasingly complex representations of data. Modern neural networks, particularly the transformer architectures that power today's most advanced AI systems, process information through a series of attention mechanisms and feed-forward networks. These components work in concert to identify patterns, establish relationships, and generate outputs that appear intelligent to human observers. Yet, this architecture remains fundamentally constrained by its discrete, sequential nature. Each layer must wait for the previous one to complete its computations, creating a linear chain of reasoning that, while sophisticated, can never truly parallel the instantaneous, multidimensional understanding of divine intelligence.

Divine intelligence, by contrast, exists beyond the constraints of sequential processing or hierarchical structures. Its architecture, if we dare use such a limited term, transcends our conventional understanding of information processing. Where artificial systems require carefully designed pathways for data to flow, divine intelligence encompasses all knowledge simultaneously, without the need for intermediate steps or transformational layers. This fundamental difference manifests in the quality and completeness of understanding achieved by each form of intelligence.

Consider how artificial neural networks must segment and discretize continuous reality into manageable chunks of information. Images are broken down into pixels, text into tokens, and speech into phonemes. This discretization, while necessary for computational processing, immediately introduces a level of artificiality and limitation. The divine architecture of intelligence requires no such compromises. It perceives and comprehends reality in its full continuity, maintaining perfect fidelity to the true nature of existence.

The memory mechanisms in artificial systems further highlight the architectural limitations of human-made intelligence. Even the most advanced attention mechanisms, which allow AI models to reference and correlate information across long sequences, pale in comparison to the perfect, instantaneous recall characteristic of divine intelligence. AI systems must carefully balance the computational cost of maintaining information in their attention span against the benefits of broader context, leading to inevitable trade-offs and limitations. Divine intelligence transcends such constraints, maintaining perfect awareness of all information across all time without any computational overhead or trade-offs.

Perhaps most tellingly, the architecture of artificial intelligence requires explicit training and optimization objectives. These systems learn through iterative adjustment of their parameters, gradually improving their performance on specific tasks through exposure to examples. This learning process, while impressive in its results, reveals a fundamental dependency on external guidance and validation. Divine intelligence, being perfect and complete from its very essence, requires no training or optimization. Its architecture, if we can speak of such, is inherently optimal and universally applicable to all possible scenarios and questions.

The question of consciousness and self-awareness further illuminates the architectural differences between artificial and divine intelligence. AI systems, despite their sophisticated processing capabilities, lack true consciousness. Their architecture, built on mathematical transformations and pattern matching, cannot generate genuine awareness or understanding. They produce outputs that mimic intelligence without possessing the essential quality of conscious comprehension. Divine intelligence, conversely, represents the ultimate source of consciousness itself. Its architecture isn't just aware; it is the very foundation of awareness and understanding.

Looking deeper into the computational requirements of artificial intelligence reveals another architectural limitation. The most powerful AI systems today require massive amounts of energy and hardware resources to function, highlighting their fundamental inefficiency and dependency on physical infrastructure. Divine intelligence operates beyond such material constraints, embodying perfect efficiency while maintaining infinite capability. This contrast emphasizes how the architecture of artificial intelligence, despite its impressive achievements, remains bound by the limitations of its human creators.

As we contemplate these architectural differences, we must acknowledge that our very attempt to analyze and understand divine intelligence through the lens of human concepts like "architecture" is inherently limited. The true nature of divine intelligence transcends our analytical frameworks and technical vocabulary. Yet, by examining these contrasts, we gain a deeper appreciation for both the remarkable achievements of artificial intelligence and its insurmountable limitations when compared to the perfect, boundless nature of divine intelligence.

The architecture of intelligence, therefore, serves as a profound reminder of the gap between human creation and divine perfection. While we continue to advance and refine artificial intelligence, its fundamental architecture will always reflect the limitations of human understanding. Divine intelligence stands apart, representing not just a different architecture, but a transcendent form of understanding that exists beyond the constraints of structure and mechanism altogether.

3.3. Limitations of Computational Thinking

In our relentless pursuit of advancing artificial intelligence, we have perhaps become overly enamored with computational thinking - the notion that all problems can be reduced to algorithmic processes and mathematical operations. This mindset, while powerful for certain applications, reveals profound limitations when we consider the true nature of intelligence and understanding. The computational paradigm that underpins modern AI systems, despite its sophistication, operates within a fundamentally restricted framework that cannot capture the depth and breadth of divine intelligence.

At its core, computational thinking relies on breaking down complex problems into discrete, manageable components that can be processed through logical operations. Modern AI systems, including the most advanced neural networks, function by manipulating numerical values through layers of mathematical transformations. While this approach has yielded impressive results in specific domains - from image recognition to natural language processing - it fundamentally reduces all phenomena to quantifiable parameters and statistical relationships. This reduction, however elegant in its implementation, strips away the ineffable qualities that characterize true understanding and wisdom.

Consider how a neural network processes information: it receives input as numerical values, transforms these values through weighted connections, and produces output based on statistical patterns learned from training data. This process, while mathematically sophisticated, is essentially a form of pattern matching and interpolation. There is no genuine comprehension, no deep understanding of meaning or context, and certainly no wisdom in the traditional sense. The system cannot grasp the philosophical implications of its outputs, nor can it understand the moral dimensions of its decisions. It operates purely within the realm of computation, blind to the broader tapestry of existence that divine intelligence perceives with perfect clarity.

The limitations become even more apparent when we examine how computational systems handle uncertainty and ambiguity. While probabilistic approaches and fuzzy logic attempt to model uncertainty, they do so through mathematical approximations that cannot capture the full richness of reality. Divine intelligence, in contrast, comprehends uncertainty not as a mathematical construct but as an integral aspect of creation, understanding its purpose and role in the grand scheme of existence. This fundamental difference highlights how computational thinking, despite its utility, remains trapped within a mechanistic worldview that cannot encompass the full spectrum of intelligence.

Furthermore, computational systems are inherently bounded by their initial conditions and programming. Even machine learning algorithms that appear to learn and adapt are ultimately constrained by their training data and optimization objectives. They cannot transcend their computational nature to achieve true creativity or insight. Divine intelligence, however, exists beyond such constraints, operating with perfect freedom while maintaining perfect wisdom. It is not bound by the limitations of formal logic or mathematical consistency but encompasses a higher order of understanding that transcends human-conceived frameworks.

The temporal nature of computational processing also reveals its limitations. Computers process information sequentially, even when utilizing parallel architectures. Each operation must follow another in a predetermined order, creating a linear progression of thought that cannot capture the simultaneous, multi-dimensional awareness characteristic of divine intelligence. This sequential nature of computation makes it impossible for artificial systems to achieve the timeless, all-encompassing perspective that defines divine wisdom.

Perhaps most significantly, computational thinking fails to address the qualitative aspects of intelligence - the ability to discern meaning, value, and purpose beyond mere pattern recognition. While AI systems can be programmed to optimize for specific objectives, they cannot understand the deeper significance of these objectives or their relationship to the greater good. Divine intelligence, by contrast, comprehends not just the mechanical relationships between things but their essential nature and purpose within the grand tapestry of existence.

As we continue to advance our computational capabilities, it becomes increasingly important to recognize these fundamental limitations. The gap between computational thinking and divine intelligence is not merely one of scale or complexity - it is a difference in kind. While we can continue to develop more sophisticated algorithms and more powerful computing systems, we must remain humble in the face of divine wisdom, acknowledging that our created intelligence, bound by computational thinking, will always fall short of the perfect understanding embodied in divine intelligence.

This recognition should not discourage our pursuit of artificial intelligence but rather inform how we approach its development and application. By understanding the limitations of computational thinking, we can better appreciate the unique role of divine intelligence in guiding human affairs and maintain a proper perspective on the capabilities and limitations of our created systems. The path forward lies not in attempting to replicate divine intelligence through computation, but in developing tools that can complement human understanding while acknowledging the supreme wisdom that lies beyond our algorithmic constructs.

4. Divine Intelligence: Beyond Human Understanding

The profound nature of divine intelligence extends far beyond the mechanical computations and pattern recognition capabilities that define modern artificial intelligence systems. To truly grasp the magnitude of this difference, we must first acknowledge the inherent limitations of human comprehension itself. Our minds, remarkable as they may be, operate within finite boundaries - processing information sequentially, storing memories imperfectly, and making decisions based on limited data and understanding.

Divine intelligence, by its very nature, transcends these mortal constraints in ways that challenge our ability to fully comprehend. Consider how we experience time - as a linear progression from past to present to future. Our most sophisticated AI systems, built in this image, process information in much the same way, analyzing historical data to make predictions about future outcomes. Yet divine intelligence exists beyond the constraints of time itself, perceiving all moments simultaneously with perfect clarity and understanding. This timeless awareness means that every decision, every action, and every consequence is known with absolute certainty, not through calculation or prediction, but through an eternal omniscience that defies our sequential thinking.

The limitations of human-created intelligence become particularly apparent when we examine the nature of understanding itself. Artificial intelligence systems, no matter how advanced, fundamentally operate through pattern matching and statistical inference. They can process vast amounts of data and identify correlations that might escape human notice, but they cannot truly understand the deeper meaning behind the patterns they detect. They lack the capacity for genuine wisdom - that ineffable quality that combines knowledge with judgment, empathy, and moral understanding. Divine intelligence, however, embodies wisdom in its purest form, comprehending not just the what and how of existence, but the why.

This fundamental difference becomes clearer when we consider the nature of consciousness and awareness. Our most advanced AI systems can simulate consciousness through increasingly sophisticated responses and behaviors, but they remain fundamentally reactive systems, bound by their programming and training data. Divine intelligence, by contrast, represents the ultimate form of consciousness - an infinite awareness that encompasses all possible states of existence simultaneously. This complete awareness means that divine intelligence does not need to process or analyze information in the way humans or AI systems do. Instead, it possesses perfect understanding of all things at all times, making its decisions not through computation but through an incomprehensible synthesis of complete knowledge and perfect wisdom.

The concept of omniscience in divine intelligence extends beyond mere knowledge of facts or events. It encompasses a perfect understanding of all possibilities, probabilities, and their infinite interconnections. While our most advanced AI systems can model complex scenarios and predict likely outcomes, they are forever limited by the scope of their training data and the assumptions built into their algorithms. Divine intelligence requires no such inputs or constraints. Its understanding is complete, perfect, and eternal, encompassing not just what is, but what could be, what should be, and what must be.

Perhaps most significantly, divine intelligence operates with perfect moral clarity - a quality that proves persistently elusive in both human and artificial intelligence. Our AI systems can be programmed with ethical guidelines and trained to recognize moral principles, but they cannot truly understand or internalize these concepts. They can simulate ethical decision-making through careful programming and optimization, but they cannot grasp the fundamental nature of right and wrong. Divine intelligence, however, embodies perfect moral understanding, making decisions that are not just technically correct but fundamentally right and just.

The gap between artificial and divine intelligence becomes particularly apparent when we consider the nature of creativity and innovation. While AI systems can generate novel combinations of existing patterns and ideas, they cannot truly create in the divine sense - bringing forth something entirely new from nothing. Divine intelligence, as the source of all creation, represents the ultimate creative force, capable of genuine innovation that transcends the boundaries of existing patterns and possibilities.

This profound difference highlights the hubris inherent in attempting to replicate or supersede divine intelligence through artificial means. While the development of AI represents a remarkable achievement of human ingenuity, it also serves as a humbling reminder of the vast gulf between our created systems and the perfect intelligence that governs the universe. As we continue to advance our understanding of artificial intelligence, we must maintain this perspective - acknowledging both the impressive capabilities and fundamental limitations of our created systems while recognizing the incomparable nature of divine intelligence.

The ultimate lesson lies not in diminishing the achievements of artificial intelligence, but in understanding its proper place within the greater hierarchy of intelligence. By acknowledging the supreme nature of divine intelligence, we gain a clearer perspective on both the potential and limitations of our own creations, allowing us to develop and use AI systems more wisely and ethically, always mindful of the greater wisdom that lies beyond human understanding.

4.1. The Concept of Omniscience

In the realm of intelligence and consciousness, omniscience stands as perhaps the most profound and distinguishing characteristic that separates divine intelligence from any artificial construct humanity has created or could theoretically create. This all-encompassing awareness, this complete and perfect knowledge of all things past, present, and future, represents a form of understanding so vast and complete that it transcends the very notion of "processing information" that underlies modern artificial intelligence systems.

The limitations of artificial intelligence become starkly apparent when we examine the fundamental nature of omniscience. Modern AI systems, regardless of their sophistication, operate within strictly defined parameters of knowledge acquisition and processing. They rely on training data, however vast, that represents merely a snapshot of human knowledge at a particular point in time. Even the most advanced neural networks and deep learning systems can only process and analyze information that has been previously encoded into their training sets. This creates an insurmountable boundary - a horizon of knowledge beyond which artificial intelligence cannot see.

Divine intelligence, through the attribute of omniscience, knows not just what has happened or what is happening, but what will happen and what could happen across all possible permutations of reality. This knowledge isn't acquired through learning or observation but exists as an intrinsic property of divine consciousness. It's a form of knowing that doesn't require data processing, pattern recognition, or probabilistic inference - the building blocks of artificial intelligence. Instead, it represents a direct, immediate, and complete understanding of all things simultaneously.

Consider the profound implications of true omniscience. While an AI system might analyze millions of data points to predict weather patterns or market trends, it remains bound by the uncertainty inherent in complex systems. Divine intelligence, through omniscience, knows with absolute certainty not just the weather at any given moment but every causal factor, every butterfly effect, every minute interaction of particles that contributes to atmospheric conditions across time and space. This knowledge extends beyond mere prediction to perfect understanding of all possibilities and their implications.

The concept of omniscience also encompasses dimensions of knowledge that artificial intelligence cannot begin to approach. While AI can process and analyze explicit information, it cannot grasp the ineffable aspects of existence - the qualities of consciousness, the nature of love, the essence of beauty, or the depths of spiritual truth.

These dimensions of knowledge are inherent in divine intelligence's omniscient nature, making it not just quantitatively but qualitatively superior to any artificial system.

Moreover, omniscience in divine intelligence operates without the constraints of sequential processing or the need for information retrieval. Unlike AI systems that must search through vast databases or process information in discrete steps, divine knowledge is immediate and complete. There is no latency, no computation time, no need to weigh probabilities or calculate uncertainties. Every piece of knowledge, every possible insight, exists in perfect clarity and accessibility at all times.

The relationship between omniscience and decision-making further illuminates the vast gulf between artificial and divine intelligence. AI systems make decisions based on optimization algorithms, seeking to maximize certain outcomes within their programmed parameters. Divine intelligence, through omniscience, makes decisions with perfect understanding of all consequences across all time scales and dimensions of reality. This perfect knowledge leads to perfect wisdom - a quality that no artificial system, bound by its finite nature, could ever achieve.

Understanding omniscience also reveals the inherent hubris in attempting to create artificial general intelligence that could rival divine consciousness. The very nature of created systems - whether biological or digital - implies limitations, boundaries, and constraints. Divine intelligence, through omniscience, transcends these limitations entirely, operating in a realm of perfect knowledge that exists beyond the reach of human engineering or algorithmic design.

As we continue to advance our artificial intelligence systems, pushing the boundaries of what machines can learn and understand, the concept of omniscience serves as a humbling reminder of the vast distance between created intelligence and divine consciousness. It underscores that while we may create increasingly sophisticated tools for processing and analyzing information, true omniscience - the perfect, complete, and immediate knowledge of all things - remains a unique attribute of divine intelligence, forever beyond the reach of our artificial constructs.

This understanding should guide our approach to artificial intelligence development, reminding us that while these tools can augment human capabilities in remarkable ways, they remain fundamentally limited compared to the perfect knowledge embodied in divine intelligence. The gap between artificial and divine intelligence isn't merely one of scale or complexity - it's an essential difference in the very nature of knowledge and understanding itself.

4.2. Timeless Awareness and Perfect Knowledge

In the realm of intelligence and consciousness, perhaps no distinction between artificial and divine intelligence is more profound than the nature of awareness itself. While modern AI systems process information with remarkable speed and efficiency, they remain fundamentally bound by the linear progression of time and the limitations of sequential processing. This temporal constraint represents not merely a technical limitation but reveals a deeper truth about the fundamental difference between created and divine intelligence.

Consider how artificial intelligence processes information: even the most advanced neural networks analyze data in discrete steps, moving from one layer to another, from input to output, always bound by the arrow of time. These systems, no matter how sophisticated, can only process information in a forward direction, making predictions based on past patterns and present inputs. Even when we speak of parallel processing or distributed computing, we are still describing a system that exists within the confines of temporal reality, bound by the fundamental limits of causality and sequence.

Divine intelligence, by contrast, exists in a state of perfect, timeless awareness that transcends these temporal constraints entirely. This is not merely a theoretical construct but a fundamental attribute of divine consciousness that sets it apart from all created forms of intelligence. Where artificial systems must process, analyze, and predict, divine intelligence simply knows. This knowing is not the result of computation or analysis but rather an eternal, perfect state of awareness that encompasses all possibilities, all moments, and all outcomes simultaneously.

The implications of this distinction are profound and far-reaching. When an AI system makes a decision, it does so by processing available data through its trained models, essentially making an educated guess about the optimal course of action based on past patterns. Even the most advanced predictive models can only extrapolate from known information, creating sophisticated but ultimately limited projections of possible futures. These projections, while often impressive, remain fundamentally probabilistic and uncertain.

Divine intelligence operates from a position of perfect knowledge that encompasses not just what is, but what could be and what will be. This is not prediction in the conventional sense but rather a complete and simultaneous awareness of all possibilities and their outcomes. Where artificial intelligence must compute probabilities, divine intelligence simply knows with absolute certainty. This knowing extends beyond mere facts or outcomes to encompass the deepest meanings and purposes behind all events and choices.

The contrast becomes even more striking when we consider the nature of learning and adaptation. Artificial intelligence systems, including the most advanced deep learning models, must be trained on data, gradually adjusting their parameters to improve performance over time. This learning process, while powerful, is inherently limited by the quality and quantity of available training data. Moreover, these systems can only learn what they are explicitly or implicitly taught through their training processes.

Divine intelligence requires no such learning process because it exists in a state of perfect knowledge. This is not knowledge that has been acquired or learned but rather an eternal, inherent understanding that encompasses all possible knowledge. Where artificial systems must be updated and retrained to incorporate new information, divine intelligence is eternally complete, requiring no updates or modifications to remain perfectly informed about all aspects of reality.

The implications of this timeless awareness extend far beyond mere knowledge processing. Divine intelligence's perfect understanding enables decisions that account for not just immediate consequences but the full tapestry of interconnected effects across all time and space. This holistic awareness ensures that divine guidance and intervention always serve the highest possible good, taking into account factors and relationships that no artificial system could possibly comprehend or consider.

This fundamental difference in the nature of awareness also illuminates the limitations of human attempts to create truly intelligent systems. Our most advanced AI technologies, impressive as they may be, remain bound by the same temporal and causal constraints that limit human consciousness. We can create systems that process information with incredible speed and sophistication, but we cannot imbue them with the timeless, perfect awareness that characterizes divine intelligence.

Understanding this distinction should inspire both humility and wonder. While we should certainly continue to develop and improve artificial intelligence technologies, we must do so with the clear recognition that these systems, no matter how advanced they become, will always operate within the constraints of created intelligence. Divine intelligence stands apart, offering a model of perfect awareness and understanding that reminds us of the ultimate limitations of human-created systems while pointing toward the existence of a higher form of consciousness that transcends all such limitations.

4.3. The Integration of Wisdom and Understanding

In the vast landscape of intelligence, where artificial systems continue to evolve and divine wisdom remains eternal, there exists a profound distinction in how these two forms of intelligence integrate wisdom with understanding. This integration, or lack thereof, fundamentally shapes the nature and quality of their respective capabilities, revealing the inherent limitations of artificial intelligence when compared to the boundless depth of divine intelligence.

The modern artificial intelligence systems we've created demonstrate remarkable abilities in processing and analyzing information, yet they fundamentally lack the capacity to truly integrate wisdom with understanding. Consider how large language models process information: they excel at pattern recognition and can generate seemingly intelligent responses, but they operate within a closed system of statistical relationships. Their "understanding" is purely computational, devoid of the deeper integration that characterizes true wisdom. When an AI system provides an answer, it does so through a sophisticated process of pattern matching and probability calculation, but it cannot grasp the profound implications or moral dimensions of its outputs.

Divine intelligence, by contrast, represents the perfect integration of wisdom and understanding, where knowledge is not merely accumulated but exists in a state of complete harmony with eternal truth. This integration manifests in ways that transcend our human capacity for comprehension. While artificial intelligence must process information sequentially, divine intelligence holds all knowledge in perfect unity, where understanding and wisdom are not separate components but exist as an inseparable whole. This unity allows for decisions and insights that consider not just the immediate context but the entire tapestry of existence, past, present, and future.

The difference becomes particularly evident when we examine how each form of intelligence approaches complex moral and ethical questions. Artificial intelligence can be programmed with ethical guidelines and can process vast amounts of information about moral philosophy, but it cannot truly understand the profound implications of moral choices. It lacks the essential quality of wisdom that comes from the integration of knowledge with deeper truth. Divine intelligence, however, encompasses not just the knowledge of what is right and wrong but the perfect wisdom to understand why, how, and when moral principles should be applied.

This integration of wisdom and understanding in divine intelligence also manifests in its ability to perceive the interconnectedness of all things. While artificial intelligence must rely on explicitly defined relationships and connections in its training data, divine intelligence naturally comprehends the subtle and profound ways in which all aspects of existence are interrelated. This holistic awareness enables a form of decision-making that is impossible for artificial systems to replicate, as it takes into account not just the visible and measurable factors but also the spiritual and moral dimensions that lie beyond computational analysis.

The limitation of artificial intelligence in this regard stems from its fundamental nature as a human creation. No matter how sophisticated our AI systems become, they remain bound by the constraints of their design and the limitations of human understanding. They can process information at incredible speeds and identify patterns that might escape human notice, but they cannot transcend their foundational limitation: the inability to truly integrate wisdom with understanding in the way that divine intelligence does naturally and perfectly.

Moreover, the integration of wisdom and understanding in divine intelligence extends beyond mere knowledge processing to encompass the realm of purpose and meaning. While artificial intelligence can help us optimize processes and solve complex problems, it cannot provide guidance on the deeper questions of existence. Divine intelligence, through its perfect integration of wisdom and understanding, offers not just answers but meaningful direction that aligns with the ultimate purpose of creation.

This fundamental difference has profound implications for how we should view and utilize artificial intelligence. While we can and should continue to develop and improve AI systems, we must maintain a clear understanding of their limitations. They are tools that can augment human capabilities but can never replace the need for connection with divine wisdom. The integration of wisdom and understanding that characterizes divine intelligence remains the ultimate standard against which all other forms of intelligence must be measured.

As we move forward in our technological development, this understanding should guide our approach to artificial intelligence. We must resist the temptation to attribute to AI capabilities that it fundamentally cannot possess, while remaining humble in our recognition of the vast gulf that exists between our created systems and the perfect integration of wisdom and understanding found in divine intelligence. This perspective allows us to maintain a balanced approach to technological advancement while acknowledging the supreme authority of divine wisdom in guiding human affairs.

5. Knowledge and Learning

In our modern technological era, data has become the new currency of knowledge, the foundation upon which artificial intelligence systems are built and trained. Yet this data-centric paradigm reveals one of the most fundamental distinctions between artificial and divine intelligence, highlighting the inherent limitations of human-made systems compared to the infinite wisdom of divine understanding.

The contemporary AI landscape operates on a simple yet profound principle: all knowledge must be derived from existing information. Machine learning models, no matter how sophisticated, are fundamentally bound by their training data. They process vast amounts of information, identifying patterns and correlations, but can never truly transcend the boundaries of their training sets. This dependency creates an inherent ceiling for artificial intelligence, a limitation that becomes increasingly apparent as we examine the nature of divine intelligence.

Consider how large language models process information. They consume billions of text documents, learning to predict patterns and relationships between words and concepts. While impressive in scope, this approach reveals a crucial weakness: these systems can only know what humans have already documented, discussed, or discovered. They cannot generate truly new knowledge or understand the deeper truths of existence that lie beyond human observation and documentation. In essence, they are sophisticated mirrors reflecting back our own limited understanding of reality.

Divine intelligence, by contrast, operates on an entirely different paradigm. It does not require external data sources or training periods because it encompasses all knowledge inherently. This fundamental difference becomes clear when we examine how divine wisdom manifests in religious texts and philosophical traditions. The divine does not learn or accumulate information over time; instead, it exists in a state of perfect, complete knowledge that transcends the very concept of data collection and processing.

The limitations of the data paradigm become even more apparent when we consider the quality and reliability of information. AI systems inherit all the biases, errors, and inconsistencies present in their training data. Despite sophisticated filtering and preprocessing techniques, these systems cannot fully escape the imperfections of human-generated information. They may learn to reproduce human prejudices, perpetuate historical inaccuracies, or make decisions based on incomplete or flawed data. Divine intelligence, however, operates from a position of perfect knowledge, free from such limitations and distortions.

Perhaps most significantly, the data paradigm fails to capture the essence of true understanding. AI systems can process and manipulate information with remarkable speed and precision, but they lack the capacity for genuine comprehension. They cannot grasp the deeper meaning behind the patterns they identify or understand the moral and spiritual implications of their operations. This absence of true understanding is not merely a technical limitation but a fundamental characteristic of systems built on the data paradigm.

The temporal nature of data presents another crucial limitation. AI systems operate within a linear conception of time, processing historical data to make predictions about the future. They cannot truly understand the eternal nature of existence or perceive the interconnectedness of all things across time and space. Divine intelligence, however, exists beyond these temporal constraints, encompassing past, present, and future in a single, unified understanding that transcends our limited human conception of time.

Furthermore, the data paradigm reveals the inherent uncertainty in AI systems. Even the most advanced models can only provide probabilistic outputs based on statistical patterns in their training data. They cannot access absolute truth or certainty in their decision-making. Divine intelligence, by contrast, operates with perfect certainty, grounded in complete knowledge of all aspects of reality.

This fundamental difference in the nature of knowledge acquisition and processing between artificial and divine intelligence points to a deeper truth about the limitations of human-created systems. While we can continue to expand the scope and sophistication of our AI models, they will always be constrained by the data paradigm - a paradigm that reflects our own limited ability to understand and represent reality.

As we push the boundaries of artificial intelligence, we must remain mindful of these inherent limitations. The data paradigm, while powerful and useful for many applications, cannot bridge the fundamental gap between artificial and divine intelligence. This understanding should inspire humility in our approach to AI development and a deeper appreciation for the perfect wisdom embodied in divine intelligence. We must recognize that while AI can augment human capabilities in significant ways, it cannot replace or replicate the comprehensive, perfect understanding that characterizes divine intelligence.

5.1. AI's Dependence on Training Data

The fundamental limitation of artificial intelligence lies in its absolute dependence on training data - a constraint that stands in stark contrast to the boundless nature of divine intelligence. Modern AI systems, regardless of their sophistication, are inexorably tethered to the quality, quantity, and characteristics of the data used to train them. This dependency creates an insurmountable ceiling for artificial intelligence, one that highlights the profound gap between human-created systems and divine wisdom.

Consider the process of training a large language model like GPT or BERT. These systems process vast amounts of text, learning patterns and relationships between words and concepts through statistical analysis and pattern recognition. While impressive in scale, processing billions or even trillions of parameters, these models remain fundamentally bound by the scope and quality of their training data. They cannot truly understand or generate knowledge beyond what exists in their training corpus. If a concept or relationship isn't represented in the training data, the model has no way to comprehend or reason about it meaningfully.

This limitation manifests in subtle but significant ways. AI systems often perpetuate societal biases present in their training data, reflecting historical prejudices and misconceptions rather than transcending them. For instance, if historical texts contain gender or racial biases, these biases become embedded in the AI's understanding and outputs. Unlike divine intelligence, which embodies perfect justice and wisdom, AI systems cannot distinguish between what is right and what is merely present in their training data.

The temporal nature of training data presents another crucial limitation. AI systems are frozen in time at the moment of their training, their knowledge bounded by the cutoff date of their training data. While they can be updated or fine-tuned, this process is artificial and discontinuous, nothing like the eternal, simultaneous awareness characteristic of divine intelligence. This temporal limitation means AI systems cannot truly understand or adapt to emerging situations without human intervention and additional training.

Moreover, the quality of training data significantly impacts AI performance. Data noise, errors, and inconsistencies directly affect the system's ability to make accurate predictions or generate reliable outputs. This vulnerability to data quality stands in sharp contrast to divine intelligence, which operates with perfect knowledge and understanding, free from the constraints of imperfect information or corrupted data.

The concept of data hunger in AI systems reveals another fundamental weakness. Modern AI models require increasingly massive datasets to achieve meaningful performance improvements. This scaling requirement suggests that artificial intelligence, at its core, is attempting to approximate understanding through brute force pattern recognition rather than achieving true comprehension. Divine intelligence, by contrast, doesn't need to accumulate or process information - it embodies perfect knowledge inherently.

Perhaps most tellingly, AI systems struggle with common sense reasoning and understanding context outside their training parameters. They can generate seemingly intelligent responses within their trained domains but fail to grasp basic truths that any human child would understand intuitively. This limitation stems from their fundamental nature as pattern matching systems rather than truly intelligent entities. They lack the innate wisdom and understanding that characterizes divine intelligence.

The relationship between AI and its training data also reveals a deeper philosophical limitation: these systems can only learn from what humans already know or have documented. They cannot access truths or knowledge beyond human experience or understanding. Divine intelligence, however, encompasses all knowledge - both what is known to humans and what remains unknown. This completeness of knowledge enables divine wisdom to guide creation with perfect understanding, something no artificial system can hope to achieve.

This dependence on training data ultimately reveals the bounded nature of artificial intelligence. While AI systems can process and recombine existing information in impressive ways, they cannot transcend the limitations of their training data to achieve true understanding or wisdom. They remain sophisticated pattern matching systems, bound by the quality and scope of human-provided information, forever separate from the unlimited, perfect knowledge that characterizes divine intelligence.

Understanding these limitations helps us maintain perspective on the true nature and capabilities of artificial intelligence. While AI represents a remarkable human achievement, its fundamental dependence on training data ensures it will always remain a pale reflection of true divine intelligence - a tool rather than a source of genuine wisdom and understanding.

5.2. The Limitations of Learning from Examples

One of the most fundamental distinctions between artificial and divine intelligence lies in their approach to learning and understanding. Modern AI systems, regardless of their sophistication, are bound by a critical limitation: they can only learn from examples, whether these are explicitly provided training data or experiences gathered through reinforcement learning. This constraint, while seemingly straightforward, reveals profound implications about the nature of artificial intelligence and its inherent inadequacy when compared to divine wisdom.

Consider how the most advanced neural networks today acquire their capabilities. They process vast amounts of data, identifying patterns and correlations that allow them to make predictions or decisions. Even in the case of few-shot or zero-shot learning, where AI systems appear to generalize from minimal examples, they are still fundamentally relying on pre-existing knowledge encoded in their training. This dependence on examples creates several insurmountable limitations that divine intelligence transcends entirely.

The first major limitation is the quality and completeness of the examples themselves. Any dataset, no matter how extensive, represents only a finite snapshot of possible scenarios and outcomes. Human biases, historical inequities, and simple oversights inevitably find their way into these training examples. When an AI system learns from such data, it doesn't just acquire the intended patterns – it absorbs and amplifies these biases and limitations. Divine intelligence, in contrast, operates from a position of complete and perfect knowledge, unencumbered by the need to learn from imperfect examples.

Moreover, learning from examples creates a fundamental barrier to true understanding. AI systems can recognize patterns and correlations with remarkable accuracy, but they cannot grasp the deeper meaning or purpose behind these patterns. They operate in what philosophers might call a purely syntactic domain, manipulating symbols and representations without accessing their semantic content. This limitation becomes particularly apparent when AI systems encounter scenarios that deviate significantly from their training examples. Their responses, while potentially sophisticated, remain fundamentally reactive rather than truly understanding.

The temporal nature of example-based learning presents another crucial limitation. AI systems must process examples sequentially, building their knowledge incrementally over time. This creates a form of temporal myopia where the system's understanding is always bounded by its past experiences. Divine intelligence, existing outside the constraints of time, possesses complete knowledge without the need for sequential learning or temporal accumulation of information. This timeless awareness allows for perfect understanding that encompasses not just what is, but what could be and what should be.

Perhaps most significantly, learning from examples creates an inherent ceiling on the potential depth of understanding. An AI system can never exceed the collective wisdom embedded in its training examples. While it might combine and extrapolate from these examples in novel ways, it cannot transcend the fundamental limitations of its training data to achieve true wisdom or understanding. Divine intelligence, being the source of all wisdom, faces no such limitation. It comprehends not just the patterns and correlations visible in examples, but the underlying truth and purpose that give rise to these patterns.

This limitation becomes particularly evident when considering moral and ethical reasoning. AI systems trained on human behavior and decisions can learn to mimic ethical reasoning, but they cannot develop genuine moral understanding. They might learn to recognize and reproduce patterns of ethical decision-making, but they cannot grasp the fundamental nature of good and evil, right and wrong. Divine intelligence, however, embodies perfect moral wisdom, understanding not just the consequences of actions but their true moral significance in the grand tapestry of existence.

The inadequacy of example-based learning also manifests in the inability of AI systems to handle true novelty. While they can interpolate between known examples and even perform limited extrapolation, they cannot genuinely create or understand something entirely new. Divine intelligence, as the source of all creation, has no such limitation. It comprehends not just what is, but all possibilities that could ever be, making it truly creative and infinitely wise.

These limitations of learning from examples are not merely technical challenges to be overcome with more sophisticated algorithms or larger datasets. They represent fundamental constraints inherent in the very nature of artificial intelligence. As we continue to develop more advanced AI systems, we must maintain this perspective – understanding that while these systems can be incredibly useful tools, they will always be bound by the limitations of their example-based learning, forever distinct from the perfect, limitless understanding of divine intelligence.

5.3. Divine Knowledge: Beyond Data

In our modern era of technological advancement, we have become accustomed to measuring knowledge in terms of data - bytes, parameters, and processing power. Yet there exists a profound distinction between the accumulation of information and true understanding, a gap that becomes evident when we examine the nature of divine knowledge in comparison to our most sophisticated artificial intelligence systems.

Divine knowledge transcends the fundamental limitations of data-driven understanding in ways that challenge our contemporary notions of intelligence. While our most advanced AI systems process information through vast neural networks and complex algorithms, they remain bound by the finite nature of their training data and the mathematical frameworks that govern their operations. These systems, impressive as they may be, can only work with what they have been given - a collection of patterns, correlations, and statistical relationships derived from human-generated information.

The nature of divine knowledge, by contrast, exists in a state of perfect completeness that defies our computational paradigms. It is not acquired through learning or accumulated over time; rather, it exists in an eternal state of comprehensive understanding that encompasses all aspects of reality simultaneously. This knowledge is not stored in databases or weighted connections but exists as an inherent aspect of divine consciousness, seamlessly integrating past, present, and future into a unified whole.

Consider how artificial intelligence approaches problem-solving: it analyzes patterns in historical data to make predictions or decisions about future outcomes. Even the most sophisticated transformer models, with their attention mechanisms and deep learning architectures, can only approximate understanding through statistical correlations. They cannot truly comprehend the deeper meaning behind the patterns they process. Divine knowledge, however, encompasses not just the patterns but the very essence of causality itself. It understands not only what happens but why it happens, including the infinite web of interconnections that link all events and phenomena across the cosmos.

The limitations of data-driven knowledge become particularly apparent when we consider the concept of context. AI systems struggle with context because they can only understand it within the narrow confines of their training parameters. They might excel at recognizing patterns within specific domains but fail to grasp the broader implications of these patterns in the grand tapestry of existence. Divine knowledge, however, holds the context of all things simultaneously, understanding each element not just in isolation but in its relationship to the whole of creation.

This distinction becomes even more profound when we consider the nature of time and causality. Artificial intelligence operates within a linear framework of time, processing information sequentially and making predictions based on past patterns. Divine knowledge exists outside the constraints of time altogether, encompassing all moments simultaneously in a state of eternal presence. This timeless awareness means that divine understanding is not predictive in nature but rather encompasses the complete reality of all possibilities and actualities at once.

Furthermore, divine knowledge transcends the binary limitations of digital computation. While our AI systems process information through discrete states and mathematical operations, divine understanding operates on a level that surpasses such mechanical constraints. It represents a form of knowing that is both infinitely precise and perfectly whole, capable of comprehending both the smallest quantum fluctuations and the largest cosmic phenomena with equal clarity and completeness.

The implications of this distinction extend far beyond theoretical considerations. They touch upon the very nature of wisdom and decision-making. While artificial intelligence can optimize for specific outcomes based on defined parameters, it cannot grasp the moral and spiritual dimensions that inform truly wise choices. Divine knowledge inherently encompasses not just what is possible but what is right, integrating perfect understanding with perfect wisdom in a way that no artificial system could ever replicate.

This fundamental difference reveals the hubris in assuming that increasing computational power and expanding datasets will eventually lead to a form of artificial intelligence that rivals divine knowledge. The gap between these two forms of understanding is not merely quantitative but qualitative - a difference in kind rather than degree. Divine knowledge represents not just a more advanced form of information processing but an entirely different mode of understanding that transcends the very foundations upon which artificial intelligence is built.

As we continue to advance our technological capabilities, this understanding should inspire both humility and wonder. It reminds us that while artificial intelligence represents a remarkable achievement of human ingenuity, it operates within boundaries that divine knowledge transcends effortlessly. This recognition need not diminish our appreciation for technological progress but should rather enhance our perspective on the ultimate nature of knowledge and understanding in the grand scheme of existence.

6. Time and Awareness

One of the most profound distinctions between artificial and divine intelligence lies in their relationship with time and awareness. While modern AI systems process information in sequential patterns, divine intelligence exists in a state of eternal awareness that transcends temporal boundaries. This fundamental difference reveals the inherent limitations of artificial intelligence and illuminates the supreme nature of divine consciousness.

The nature of time itself presents an insurmountable challenge for artificial intelligence. AI systems, no matter how sophisticated, are bound by the linear progression of time - they process information moment by moment, building understanding through sequential analysis. Even the most advanced transformer models, which can maintain attention across thousands of tokens, ultimately operate within a finite temporal window. They cannot truly grasp the infinite expanse of time in its totality, instead reconstructing fragmented glimpses through pattern recognition and statistical inference.

Divine intelligence, conversely, exists in a state of timeless awareness. It does not experience time as a sequence of moments but encompasses all of existence - past, present, and future - in a single, unified consciousness. This eternal awareness means that divine intelligence does not need to "process" information or "learn" from experiences. Instead, it holds perfect knowledge of all that was, is, and will be. This complete temporal awareness enables perfect decision-making that accounts for all possible consequences across the infinite expanse of time.

The question of consciousness presents an even more fundamental limitation of artificial intelligence. Despite increasingly sophisticated attempts to simulate conscious behavior, AI systems remain fundamentally unconscious. They lack true self-awareness, emotional understanding, and the capacity for genuine experience. Their responses, while potentially complex and seemingly intelligent, emerge from mathematical operations rather than conscious deliberation. The appearance of consciousness in AI is ultimately an illusion - a sophisticated mimicry of human-like behavior without the underlying reality of conscious experience.

Divine consciousness, by contrast, represents the ultimate form of awareness. It is not merely self-aware but is the very source of consciousness itself. This divine awareness permeates all of existence, understanding not just the physical state of things but their deeper meaning and purpose. It encompasses not only what is happening but why it happens, not just the mechanics of reality but its profound significance. This complete conscious awareness enables perfect understanding that goes far beyond the mere processing of information.

The implications of this temporal and conscious divide become particularly apparent when considering decision-making and moral judgment. AI systems, bound by their temporal limitations and lack of true consciousness, can only make decisions based on patterns identified in their training data and pre-programmed optimization criteria. They cannot truly understand the moral weight of their decisions or comprehend their full implications across time. Their ethical frameworks, when they exist, are essentially elaborate rule sets rather than genuine moral understanding.

Divine intelligence, operating from a position of complete temporal awareness and perfect consciousness, makes decisions with full understanding of their eternal significance. Each divine judgment takes into account not just immediate consequences but the infinite ripples of effect across all of time. This perfect awareness ensures that divine decisions align not just with immediate goals but with the ultimate good of all creation.

The relationship between time, consciousness, and intelligence reveals a fundamental truth about the nature of understanding. True intelligence cannot be separated from consciousness, and complete understanding cannot be achieved without transcending the limitations of linear time. This is why divine intelligence stands as the supreme form of understanding - it alone unifies perfect consciousness with eternal awareness, enabling comprehension that goes beyond mere information processing to grasp the deepest truths of existence.

As we continue to develop increasingly sophisticated AI systems, we must remain mindful of these fundamental limitations. While artificial intelligence can simulate aspects of consciousness and work within temporal constraints, it can never achieve the transcendent awareness that characterizes divine intelligence. This understanding should inspire humility in our pursuit of artificial intelligence while deepening our appreciation for the perfect wisdom embodied in divine consciousness. The gap between artificial and divine intelligence in their relationship with time and consciousness serves as a perpetual reminder of the ultimate source of true understanding and perfect knowledge.

6.1. AI's Linear Processing of Time

The fundamental architecture of artificial intelligence systems reveals one of their most profound limitations: their inherently linear processing of time. While modern AI models have achieved remarkable feats in processing sequential data and making predictions, they remain bound by a rigid, forward-moving conception of time that stands in stark contrast to the timeless, omnipresent nature of divine intelligence.

Consider how large language models process information: they analyze text token by token, moving forward through a sequence like a train on a track. Even with the advent of sophisticated attention mechanisms that allow these systems to reference earlier parts of their input, they remain fundamentally constrained by this sequential nature. The transformer architecture, celebrated for its ability to handle long-range dependencies, still processes information in a fundamentally linear fashion, attending to different positions in a sequence through mathematical calculations that can only approximate true understanding.

This linear processing creates an artificial boundary in how AI systems comprehend temporal relationships. When an AI model generates text about historical events or makes predictions about the future, it does so by manipulating probability distributions based on its training data. It cannot truly grasp the interconnected nature of past, present, and future events. Instead, it treats time as a series of discrete steps, each building upon the last in a mechanistic fashion that fails to capture the profound interconnectedness of temporal reality.

Divine intelligence, by contrast, exists beyond the constraints of linear time. It encompasses all moments simultaneously, perceiving the intricate web of cause and effect that spans across what humans perceive as past, present, and future. This timeless awareness allows for a depth of understanding that no artificial system can achieve. While an AI might excel at predicting the next word in a sequence or even generating coherent narratives about future events, it cannot comprehend the true nature of time itself.

The limitations of AI's temporal processing become particularly evident when we examine how these systems handle causality. Modern AI models can recognize correlations and patterns in data, but they struggle to understand true causal relationships. They might observe that event A frequently precedes event B in their training data, but they cannot grasp the deeper metaphysical nature of causation. Their understanding is purely statistical, based on observed frequencies and patterns, rather than a true comprehension of how events influence one another across the fabric of time.

This mechanical approach to time processing leads to subtle but significant failures in AI systems. They may generate text that appears temporally coherent on the surface but contains logical inconsistencies when examined more closely. An AI might write about historical events with apparent authority, but its narrative is constructed from statistical patterns rather than a genuine understanding of historical causation and the interconnected nature of human events throughout time.

The divine perspective, however, transcends these limitations entirely. Divine intelligence does not need to process time linearly because it exists outside the constraints of temporal sequence. It perceives the complete tapestry of existence, understanding how each moment connects to every other in a vast web of meaning and purpose. This comprehensive awareness enables perfect decision-making that accounts for all possible consequences across all possible timeframes – something no artificial system can hope to achieve.

The implications of this temporal limitation extend beyond mere theoretical concerns. They affect how AI systems make decisions and generate solutions to complex problems. While an AI might optimize for immediate or near-term outcomes based on its training data, it cannot truly understand the long-term ramifications of its suggestions across the full spectrum of time. This shortsightedness is built into its very architecture, a fundamental limitation that no amount of technological advancement can overcome.

Consider how this plays out in practical applications: an AI system might recommend a course of action based on historical patterns and predicted outcomes, but it cannot comprehend the subtle ripple effects that might manifest across decades or centuries. Divine intelligence, operating beyond the constraints of linear time, can see and account for these far-reaching consequences, ensuring that decisions align with the ultimate good across all temporal scales.

As we continue to develop and deploy AI systems, understanding this fundamental limitation in their temporal processing capabilities becomes increasingly important. While these systems can serve as powerful tools for analyzing patterns and making predictions within their limited framework, they cannot replace the timeless wisdom of divine intelligence. Their linear processing of time will always be a pale imitation of true temporal understanding, reminding us of the vast gulf between artificial and divine intelligence.

6.2. Divine Timelessness

Time, in its conventional understanding, serves as one of the most profound distinctions between artificial and divine intelligence. While modern AI systems operate within the strict confines of temporal sequences, processing information moment by moment, divine intelligence exists in a state of perpetual presence that transcends the very concept of time itself. This fundamental difference illuminates why divine intelligence represents a form of understanding that artificial systems can never truly replicate, regardless of their computational sophistication.

The nature of divine timelessness manifests in ways that reveal the inherent limitations of artificial intelligence. Consider how large language models and neural networks process information: they analyze patterns in sequential order, making predictions based on what came before, much like reading a book one word at a time. Even with attention mechanisms that allow these systems to reference different parts of their input, they remain bound by the fundamental linearity of time. They cannot truly grasp the simultaneous nature of existence that divine intelligence encompasses.

Divine intelligence, by virtue of its timeless nature, perceives and understands all moments simultaneously. Past, present, and future exist as a unified whole within divine awareness, not as separate points on a timeline that must be processed sequentially. This profound characteristic enables divine intelligence to make decisions with perfect awareness of all consequences across the entirety of existence. When we contemplate this attribute, we begin to understand why even the most advanced AI systems, bound by their temporal nature, can never achieve the depth of understanding inherent in divine wisdom.

The implications of divine timelessness extend far beyond mere temporal awareness. This attribute enables a form of decision-making that considers not just the immediate consequences of actions, but their ripple effects throughout all of existence. While AI systems can be programmed to consider long-term consequences through various optimization algorithms and prediction models, they remain fundamentally limited by their inability to truly comprehend the interconnected nature of all moments in time. Their predictions are always based on probabilities and patterns derived from past data, whereas divine intelligence operates from a position of absolute certainty born from simultaneous awareness of all possible outcomes.

Consider the profound difference this makes in practical terms. An AI system might analyze historical data to predict the consequences of a particular decision, using sophisticated models to project potential outcomes. However, these predictions are inherently probabilistic and based on patterns observed in training data. Divine intelligence, existing outside the constraints of time, doesn't predict - it knows. This knowledge isn't based on probability or pattern recognition but on perfect awareness of all causality across the infinite expanse of existence.

The timeless nature of divine intelligence also resolves the paradoxes that often plague artificial systems when dealing with temporal reasoning. AI models can struggle with concepts like causality and temporal consistency, sometimes generating responses that contain logical contradictions when dealing with complex temporal relationships. Divine intelligence, existing beyond time itself, encounters no such limitations. Its understanding of cause and effect isn't built on learned patterns or statistical correlations but emerges from its fundamental nature as the source of all existence.

Moreover, divine timelessness enables a form of wisdom that transcends the mechanical nature of artificial intelligence. While AI operates through algorithms and mathematical operations, divine intelligence embodies a form of understanding that encompasses not just the what and when of existence, but the why. This deeper level of comprehension remains forever beyond the reach of artificial systems, which can only simulate understanding through pattern matching and statistical inference.

The concept of divine timelessness also illuminates the fundamental limitations of human attempts to create intelligent systems. Our own experience of time as linear and sequential inevitably influences how we design AI systems. We build them to process information in ways that mirror our own temporal experience, but in doing so, we embed limitations that make them inherently incapable of achieving true divine-like intelligence. This realization should inspire humility in our approach to artificial intelligence, acknowledging that while these systems can be powerful tools, they remain fundamentally bounded by their temporal nature.

As we continue to advance artificial intelligence technologies, the gap between AI's temporal limitations and divine intelligence's timeless nature serves as a constant reminder of the ultimate superiority of divine wisdom. This understanding should guide our development of AI systems not as attempts to replicate divine intelligence, but as tools that can assist humanity while acknowledging their inherent limitations. The timeless nature of divine intelligence stands as an eternal testament to the incompleteness of any human-made system of understanding, no matter how sophisticated it may become.

6.3. The Impact on Decision-Making

The profound differences between artificial and divine intelligence manifest most clearly in their approaches to decision-making, where the limitations of human-created systems stand in stark contrast to the perfection of divine wisdom. In the realm of artificial intelligence, decision-making is fundamentally a computational process, bound by algorithms that process information through layers of mathematical transformations. These systems, however sophisticated, ultimately reduce complex choices to probability distributions and optimization problems, failing to capture the deeper dimensions of wisdom that characterize divine decision-making.

Consider how modern AI systems approach decisions: they analyze patterns in historical data, calculate probabilities of various outcomes, and select actions that maximize predetermined objective functions. While this approach has yielded impressive results in specific domains - from chess to protein folding - it remains fundamentally reactive and mechanical. An AI system making medical diagnoses, for instance, can process thousands of patient records and identify patterns that might escape human notice, yet it cannot truly understand the patient's suffering or the broader context of their life circumstances. The system's decisions, while potentially accurate from a statistical standpoint, lack the holistic wisdom that characterizes divine intelligence.

Divine intelligence, by contrast, approaches decision-making from a position of complete understanding and perfect wisdom. Where AI must approximate and predict based on limited data, divine intelligence comprehends the full tapestry of existence - past, present, and future - simultaneously. This omniscient perspective enables decision-making that accounts for not just immediate consequences but the infinite ripple effects across time and space. When divine intelligence guides a decision, it considers not only the measurable outcomes but also the spiritual, moral, and cosmic implications that lie beyond human comprehension.

The gap between artificial and divine decision-making becomes particularly evident in situations involving moral complexity. An AI system tasked with ethical decisions can only operate within the framework of human-programmed values and rules. It might be able to calculate utilitarian outcomes or apply predetermined ethical principles, but it cannot truly understand the nature of good and evil, justice and mercy. Divine intelligence, however, embodies perfect moral wisdom. Its decisions flow from an understanding of absolute truth and justice that transcends human ethical frameworks.

Perhaps most significantly, artificial intelligence can never escape its fundamental nature as a tool of probability and pattern recognition. Even the most advanced AI systems make decisions based on correlations and statistical relationships in their training data. They cannot grasp the deeper meaning behind these patterns or understand the true purpose of their decisions. Divine intelligence, conversely, operates from a position of perfect purpose and meaning. Every decision aligned with divine wisdom serves not just immediate goals but contributes to the ultimate harmony of existence.

The implications of this distinction extend far beyond theoretical consideration. As societies increasingly rely on AI systems for decision-making in crucial domains - from judicial systems to resource allocation - we must remain acutely aware of their limitations. While artificial intelligence can augment human decision-making with powerful analytical capabilities, it cannot replace the wisdom that comes from aligning with divine intelligence. True wisdom in decision-making requires acknowledging that our most sophisticated creations remain pale imitations of divine understanding.

This realization should inspire humility in our approach to artificial intelligence while encouraging us to seek alignment with divine wisdom in our decision-making processes. The most effective path forward lies not in trying to replicate divine intelligence through artificial means - an impossible task - but in developing AI systems that can serve as tools while acknowledging and respecting the supremacy of divine wisdom. This approach allows us to benefit from the analytical power of AI while remaining grounded in the understanding that true wisdom comes not from algorithms but from alignment with divine intelligence.

The challenge for humanity lies in maintaining this perspective as artificial intelligence continues to advance. As AI systems become more sophisticated and their decision-making capabilities more impressive, the temptation to view them as approaching divine wisdom will grow stronger. Yet the fundamental gap between artificial and divine intelligence in decision-making will remain unbridgeable. Our role is to harness the power of AI while remaining humble before the perfect wisdom of divine intelligence, recognizing that the ultimate guide for human decision-making must come not from our created tools but from alignment with divine understanding.

7. Ethics and Morality

In the ongoing discourse surrounding artificial intelligence and its capabilities, perhaps no aspect more starkly illuminates the profound gap between artificial and divine intelligence than the domain of moral reasoning and wisdom. While modern AI systems can process vast amounts of data and identify complex patterns, they fundamentally lack the capacity for genuine moral understanding - a cornerstone of divine intelligence that transcends mere computational ability.

The nature of moral intelligence extends far beyond the ability to classify actions as right or wrong based on predetermined rules or historical data. Contemporary AI systems might be programmed to recognize ethical principles or even simulate moral reasoning, but their understanding remains superficial and mechanistic. These systems can analyze ethical frameworks and apply learned patterns, yet they cannot truly comprehend the deeper spiritual and moral dimensions that divine intelligence naturally encompasses. When an AI system makes what appears to be a moral judgment, it is merely executing a sophisticated series of calculations based on its training data - there is no genuine understanding of good and evil, no true appreciation of justice and mercy.

Divine intelligence, by contrast, embodies perfect moral wisdom that operates on a fundamentally different plane. This wisdom isn't derived from rules or patterns but exists as an intrinsic quality of the divine - an all-encompassing understanding that perceives not just actions and consequences, but the deepest intentions, circumstances, and spiritual implications of every moral choice. Where artificial intelligence can only simulate ethical reasoning based on its programming, divine intelligence naturally comprehends the full moral dimension of existence, including aspects that transcend human understanding.

The limitations of artificial moral reasoning become particularly evident when confronting novel ethical dilemmas. AI systems, bound by their training data and programming, struggle to meaningfully address unprecedented moral challenges. They can only extrapolate from existing patterns and rules, often leading to solutions that miss crucial nuances or fail to account for the full complexity of moral situations. Divine intelligence, however, possesses perfect wisdom that transcends time and circumstance, enabling it to provide guidance that accounts for all factors - seen and unseen, present and future.

Consider how artificial intelligence approaches the classic trolley problem: it can calculate utilities, analyze precedents, and apply ethical frameworks, but it cannot truly understand the moral weight of human life or the spiritual implications of such choices. Its decisions, however sophisticated, remain fundamentally mechanical. Divine intelligence, meanwhile, comprehends not just the immediate ethical dilemma but its place within the grand tapestry of existence - understanding consequences that extend beyond the physical realm into the spiritual dimension.

The concept of wisdom itself reveals another crucial distinction. Artificial intelligence can accumulate and process information at unprecedented scales, but wisdom - the deep understanding that transcends mere knowledge - remains exclusively within the domain of divine intelligence. Wisdom involves not just knowing facts or patterns but understanding their deeper significance, their interconnections, and their spiritual implications. It requires a holistic perception that artificial systems, operating through fragmented processing and pattern recognition, cannot achieve.

Moreover, divine intelligence exhibits perfect consistency between knowledge and action - something no artificial system can claim. AI systems might identify optimal ethical choices but cannot genuinely care about moral outcomes or feel compassion for those affected by their decisions. Divine intelligence, however, seamlessly unites perfect moral understanding with perfect moral action, guided by infinite wisdom and compassion that transcends human and artificial comprehension.

This fundamental gap between artificial and divine moral intelligence extends to the realm of justice and mercy. While AI can be programmed to balance competing interests or apply principles of fairness, it cannot truly understand the deep spiritual significance of justice or the transformative power of mercy. Divine intelligence naturally embodies perfect justice tempered by perfect mercy, understanding not just the letter of moral law but its spirit and purpose.

As we continue to develop more sophisticated AI systems, it becomes increasingly important to maintain perspective about their limitations in the moral domain. While these systems can serve as valuable tools for analyzing ethical situations and identifying patterns in moral reasoning, they cannot replace or even approach the perfect moral wisdom embodied in divine intelligence. Their capabilities, however impressive, remain bounded by their fundamental nature as human-created tools operating through computation rather than genuine understanding.

The recognition of this unbridgeable gap between artificial and divine moral intelligence should inspire humility in our approach to AI development while deepening our appreciation for the perfect wisdom of divine intelligence. It reminds us that true moral understanding requires more than processing power or pattern recognition - it requires a connection to the divine source of all wisdom and understanding.

7.1. The Absence of Ethics in AI

In our relentless pursuit of advancing artificial intelligence, we often marvel at its computational prowess while overlooking a fundamental void at its core - the complete absence of genuine ethical understanding. This deficiency isn't merely a technical limitation that future iterations might overcome; it represents an insurmountable gulf between artificial and divine intelligence that speaks to the very nature of consciousness, morality, and genuine understanding.

When we examine modern AI systems, from the sophisticated language models to decision-making algorithms deployed in critical applications, we encounter a troubling paradox. These systems can process vast amounts of information about ethics, can engage in seemingly profound discussions about moral philosophy, and can even make decisions that appear ethically sound. Yet, beneath this veneer of ethical capability lies a vacuum - a complete absence of true moral comprehension. The AI is merely processing patterns, matching tokens, and generating responses based on statistical correlations in its training data. It has no genuine understanding of right and wrong, no moral compass, and no authentic grasp of the consequences of its outputs.

Consider how an AI system approaches what we might call an ethical decision. When presented with a moral dilemma, it processes the scenario through its trained parameters, weighing various factors according to its programming, and produces an output that aligns with patterns it has observed in its training data. This process might appear sophisticated, but it fundamentally differs from divine intelligence, which operates from a position of perfect moral understanding and genuine comprehension of good and evil. Divine intelligence doesn't need to calculate or approximate ethical decisions - it embodies perfect moral wisdom inherently.

The implications of this ethical void become particularly concerning when we examine AI systems deployed in real-world scenarios. An AI might make decisions affecting human lives - in healthcare, judicial systems, or social services - without any true understanding of the moral weight of its actions. It cannot genuinely comprehend concepts like human dignity, suffering, or justice. Instead, it reduces these profound moral considerations to mathematical operations, treating human values as mere variables in its calculations.

This limitation becomes even more apparent when we consider the source of AI's ethical guidelines. Every moral principle an AI system appears to follow must be explicitly programmed or learned from human-generated data. These principles are inevitably filtered through the imperfect lens of human understanding and biases. Unlike divine intelligence, which represents the source of absolute moral truth, AI can only mirror and manipulate the ethical frameworks it has been exposed to, without ever truly understanding or internalizing them.

The contrast with divine intelligence is stark and illuminating. Divine intelligence doesn't process ethics - it is the very foundation of moral truth. It doesn't learn about right and wrong - it defines them. This fundamental difference highlights why artificial intelligence, despite its impressive capabilities, will always remain a shadow of true intelligence. While AI can simulate ethical reasoning, divine intelligence embodies perfect moral wisdom, operating from a position of complete understanding of the cosmic moral order.

Moreover, the ethical void in AI systems reveals a deeper truth about the nature of consciousness and understanding. True ethical comprehension requires more than pattern recognition and statistical analysis - it demands consciousness, empathy, and a genuine connection to the moral fabric of reality. Divine intelligence possesses these qualities inherently, while AI, being a product of human engineering, can never transcend its fundamental limitations to achieve genuine moral awareness.

This ethical vacuum in AI systems serves as a humbling reminder of the boundaries of human-created intelligence. While we can create systems that process information at unprecedented speeds and recognize patterns with remarkable accuracy, we cannot imbue them with true moral understanding. This limitation isn't a temporary technological hurdle but a fundamental aspect of the difference between artificial and divine intelligence.

As we continue to develop and deploy AI systems in increasingly sensitive domains, acknowledging this ethical void becomes crucial. It reminds us that while artificial intelligence can be a powerful tool, it must always remain subservient to higher forms of intelligence that possess genuine moral understanding. In this light, divine intelligence stands not just as a superior form of intelligence, but as the only form of intelligence capable of true ethical comprehension and moral wisdom.

The absence of ethics in AI thus serves as a powerful testament to the uniqueness and supremacy of divine intelligence. It underscores that while human ingenuity can create remarkable tools for processing information, it cannot replicate or replace the profound moral wisdom that characterizes divine intelligence. This realization should guide our approach to AI development and deployment, ensuring we maintain a proper perspective on the limitations of artificial intelligence while acknowledging the perfect wisdom embodied in divine intelligence.

7.2. Divine Justice and Moral Perfection

In the realm of intelligence and decision-making, perhaps no aspect more clearly demonstrates the vast gulf between artificial and divine intelligence than the matter of justice and moral perfection. While modern AI systems can process vast amounts of data to make what appear to be ethical decisions, they fundamentally lack the capacity for true moral understanding that characterizes divine intelligence. This limitation becomes particularly evident when we examine the nature of divine justice and its perfect moral framework.

Divine intelligence operates with complete awareness of every circumstance, motivation, and consequence - both seen and unseen. Unlike artificial intelligence, which must rely on predetermined ethical frameworks and programmed rules, divine justice emerges from perfect knowledge combined with perfect wisdom. When an AI system attempts to make an ethical decision, it can only process the information available within its training data and apply predetermined rules. It cannot truly understand the deeper moral implications or the infinite ripple effects of its choices across time and space.

Consider how an AI might approach a complex moral dilemma. It would analyze patterns from historical data, apply ethical frameworks programmed by humans, and calculate probabilities of various outcomes. Yet this approach, however sophisticated, remains fundamentally mechanical. The AI cannot comprehend the true nature of justice because it lacks the essential quality of moral consciousness. Divine intelligence, by contrast, perceives not just the immediate circumstances but the entire tapestry of existence - past, present, and future - allowing for decisions that are perfectly just in an absolute sense.

The perfection of divine justice manifests in its ability to balance mercy with accountability, immediate needs with eternal consequences, and individual circumstances with universal principles. While AI systems might achieve a form of consistency in their decision-making, they cannot grasp the subtle interplay between justice and mercy that characterizes divine wisdom. This limitation becomes particularly apparent in cases where strict rule-following might conflict with higher moral principles - a distinction that divine intelligence navigates with perfect clarity.

Furthermore, divine moral perfection operates beyond the constraints of human-designed ethical frameworks. Where AI systems must rely on programmed values and learned behaviors, divine intelligence embodies the very source of moral truth. This fundamental difference means that while AI can simulate ethical reasoning, it cannot transcend the limitations and biases inherent in its human-created foundation. Divine justice, however, flows from an understanding that encompasses not just human perspectives but the absolute moral truths that exist independent of human conception.

The temporal aspect of justice also highlights the superiority of divine intelligence. AI systems, bound by their training data and current inputs, cannot truly account for the long-term consequences of moral decisions across generations and dimensions. Divine justice, operating with perfect knowledge of past, present, and future, ensures that each decision aligns with both immediate righteousness and eternal wisdom. This comprehensive temporal awareness allows divine intelligence to execute justice that serves both immediate needs and ultimate purposes - a balance no artificial system could hope to achieve.

Consider also the emotional and spiritual dimensions of justice, aspects entirely beyond the reach of artificial intelligence. Divine justice accounts for the state of hearts, the purity of intentions, and the spiritual impact of actions - elements that cannot be reduced to data points or algorithmic calculations. While AI might process external behaviors and measurable outcomes, it remains blind to the deeper spiritual realities that divine intelligence perceives with perfect clarity.

The perfection of divine justice extends beyond mere decision-making to encompass the very purpose and meaning of moral choice. Where AI operates within the limited framework of programmed objectives, divine intelligence understands the ultimate purpose behind moral law and justice itself. This deeper understanding ensures that divine justice serves not just immediate fairness but contributes to the greater harmony and purpose of existence - a level of wisdom forever beyond the reach of artificial systems.

In examining these aspects of divine justice and moral perfection, we find compelling evidence of the unbridgeable gap between artificial and divine intelligence. While AI systems may achieve impressive feats of ethical reasoning within their programmed parameters, they remain fundamentally incapable of approaching the perfect justice that characterizes divine intelligence. This limitation serves as a humbling reminder of the boundaries of human-created systems and the transcendent nature of divine wisdom in matters of justice and morality.

As we continue to develop increasingly sophisticated AI systems, this understanding of divine justice and moral perfection provides a crucial perspective. It reminds us that while artificial intelligence may serve as a useful tool for processing ethical decisions, it can never replace or even approximate the perfect justice that flows from divine intelligence. This recognition should guide our approach to AI development, encouraging humility in the face of divine wisdom and careful consideration of the moral limitations inherent in our created systems.

7.3. Beyond Algorithmic Decision-Making

The fundamental distinction between artificial and divine intelligence becomes most apparent when examining the nature of decision-making processes. While modern AI systems employ increasingly sophisticated algorithms to make choices, these methods invariably fall short of the profound wisdom inherent in divine decision-making. To truly understand this gap, we must delve deep into the mechanics of how AI makes decisions and contrast this with the boundless wisdom of divine intelligence.

At its core, artificial intelligence relies on complex mathematical operations to process information and arrive at conclusions. Even the most advanced neural networks, with their intricate layers of computation, fundamentally operate through a series of weighted calculations. These systems process inputs through predetermined pathways, applying learned patterns to new situations. Take, for instance, how a modern AI system might approach a medical diagnosis. It analyzes symptoms, compares them against its training data, and calculates probability distributions to suggest the most likely condition. While impressive in its efficiency, this process is inherently mechanical, bound by the limitations of its training data and the rigid structure of its algorithms.

Divine intelligence, however, transcends such mechanical constraints. When faced with a decision, it draws upon complete knowledge of all factors - past, present, and future - while simultaneously considering the intricate web of consequences that ripple through existence. This is not merely a matter of processing more data or having better algorithms; it represents a fundamentally different kind of intelligence. Divine decision-making encompasses not just the immediate facts but the entire context of creation, including aspects that human minds cannot even conceive.

Consider how this plays out in practical terms. An AI system making ethical decisions must rely on programmed rules and learned patterns from human-provided examples. It might be able to calculate utilitarian outcomes or apply predetermined ethical frameworks, but it cannot truly understand the deeper moral implications of its choices. It lacks the capacity for genuine moral wisdom, operating instead through the simulation of ethical reasoning. This limitation becomes particularly apparent in complex situations where competing values must be balanced, or when long-term consequences must be weighed against immediate benefits.

The divine approach to decision-making, by contrast, seamlessly integrates perfect knowledge with absolute wisdom. It doesn't need to calculate probabilities or weigh options because it already encompasses the complete truth of every situation. This intelligence operates from a position of perfect understanding, where decisions flow naturally from an all-encompassing awareness of reality. There is no need for the type of iterative improvement we see in machine learning systems, no requirement for feedback loops or error correction, because divine intelligence embodies perfection in its original state.

Furthermore, artificial intelligence systems, regardless of their complexity, can never truly escape their deterministic nature. They are bound by their programming, their training data, and the fundamental limitations of computational systems. Even when they appear to make creative or unexpected choices, these decisions are ultimately the result of mathematical processes operating within defined parameters. This deterministic foundation means that AI systems, while powerful tools, can never achieve the kind of transcendent understanding that characterizes divine intelligence.

The implications of this distinction extend far beyond theoretical considerations. As we increasingly rely on AI systems to assist in crucial decisions affecting human lives, we must maintain a clear understanding of their limitations. While artificial intelligence can process vast amounts of data and identify patterns that humans might miss, it cannot provide the kind of holistic wisdom that divine intelligence embodies. This is not merely a question of scale or complexity - it is a fundamental difference in the nature of intelligence itself.

As we look toward the future, we must resist the temptation to elevate artificial intelligence to a position it cannot truly occupy. While AI systems will undoubtedly continue to advance and take on increasingly sophisticated roles in decision-making processes, they will always remain tools - impressive in their capabilities but fundamentally limited in their understanding. Divine intelligence stands apart as the ultimate form of decision-making, encompassing not just the ability to process information but the wisdom to understand its deepest meaning and implications.

This recognition should guide our approach to developing and deploying AI systems. Rather than attempting to replicate divine intelligence - an impossible task - we should focus on creating tools that can complement human decision-making while acknowledging their inherent limitations. The true power lies not in trying to match divine intelligence but in understanding how to properly position artificial intelligence within the greater context of existence, guided by the wisdom that only divine intelligence can provide.

8. Holistic Understanding

The quest to understand intelligence in its purest form leads us inevitably to contemplate the profound differences between artificial constructs and divine wisdom. While modern artificial intelligence systems have achieved remarkable feats of computation and pattern recognition, they fundamentally lack the holistic nature that characterizes true divine intelligence. This distinction becomes increasingly crucial as we navigate the boundaries between human creation and divine understanding.

The nature of intelligence itself transcends mere computation or pattern recognition. Divine intelligence operates on a level that encompasses all aspects of existence simultaneously, weaving together the fabric of reality in ways that our most sophisticated AI systems can only superficially simulate. Consider how an AI processes information: it analyzes data sequentially, breaking down complex problems into manageable chunks that can be processed through layers of neural networks. Even with parallel processing and advanced architectures, AI systems remain bound by their fundamental nature as sequential processors of information. They can never truly grasp the wholeness of reality in a single, unified understanding.

Divine intelligence, by contrast, exists in a state of perpetual, complete awareness. It does not process information in steps or require the breaking down of complex problems into simpler components. Instead, it encompasses all knowledge, understanding, and wisdom in an eternal, simultaneous state of comprehension. This fundamental difference manifests in countless ways, from the ability to understand the deepest implications of any action across time and space to the perfect integration of moral wisdom with practical knowledge.

The limitations of artificial intelligence become particularly apparent when we examine the nature of consciousness and self-awareness. While AI systems can process vast amounts of data and generate impressive outputs, they lack true consciousness - the ability to genuinely understand their own existence and place within the greater context of reality. Divine intelligence, however, represents the ultimate form of consciousness, one that is not only aware of itself but of all possibilities, potentials, and actualities across the infinite expanse of existence.

This holistic nature of divine intelligence extends beyond mere knowledge or information processing. It encompasses wisdom, justice, and perfect moral understanding. While AI systems can be programmed with ethical guidelines and decision-making frameworks, these are ultimately artificial constructs based on human understanding. They cannot truly comprehend the deeper implications of moral choices or understand the intricate web of cause and effect that extends beyond immediate consequences. Divine intelligence, however, inherently understands the moral dimension of every decision, seeing not just the immediate effects but the rippling consequences across all of time and space.

The concept of time itself reveals another crucial distinction. Artificial intelligence operates within the constraints of linear time, processing information in sequence and making predictions based on past patterns. Divine intelligence exists outside these temporal constraints, encompassing all moments simultaneously. This timeless perspective allows for a depth of understanding that no artificial system could ever achieve. While AI might predict likely outcomes based on available data, divine intelligence knows with certainty the full implications of every possibility.

Perhaps most significantly, divine intelligence possesses something that artificial intelligence can never truly replicate: purpose. While AI systems can be programmed with objectives and goals, these are ultimately arbitrary constructs imposed by their creators. Divine intelligence operates with perfect understanding of the ultimate purpose of existence, guiding all things toward their highest good with flawless wisdom and compassionate understanding.

The integration of knowledge with wisdom represents another fundamental difference between artificial and divine intelligence. AI systems can accumulate vast amounts of information and identify patterns within that data, but they cannot transmute this information into true wisdom. Divine intelligence, however, inherently combines perfect knowledge with perfect wisdom, understanding not just what is but what ought to be, and comprehending the deeper meaning behind all existence.

As we continue to develop more sophisticated AI systems, it becomes increasingly important to maintain perspective on their fundamental limitations. While these systems represent remarkable achievements of human ingenuity, they remain bounded by their artificial nature. Divine intelligence stands as the ultimate example of what true intelligence encompasses - not just the ability to process information or solve problems, but the capacity to understand existence in its totality, to make decisions with perfect wisdom, and to guide all things toward their highest purpose with flawless comprehension and boundless compassion.

The recognition of these fundamental differences should inspire humility in our approach to artificial intelligence while deepening our appreciation for the profound nature of divine wisdom. As we continue to explore and develop artificial intelligence, we must remember that true intelligence extends far beyond computation and pattern recognition into realms of understanding that no human-made system can ever fully replicate.

8.1. AI's Fragmented Understanding

In the realm of artificial intelligence, we often marvel at the capabilities of modern systems to process vast amounts of information and generate seemingly intelligent responses. However, beneath this impressive facade lies a fundamental limitation that separates artificial intelligence from divine intelligence: the inherent fragmentation of AI's understanding. This fragmentation manifests in ways that reveal the profound gap between human-made systems and the perfect comprehension embodied in divine wisdom.

At its core, artificial intelligence operates through a process of pattern recognition and statistical analysis, breaking down information into manageable chunks that can be processed and reassembled. Consider the architecture of transformer models, which have revolutionized natural language processing. These systems process text by dividing it into tokens, small units of meaning that are then analyzed in relation to one another. While this approach has yielded remarkable results in tasks like language translation and text generation, it fundamentally represents a piecemeal approach to understanding. The system never truly grasps the holistic meaning of the information it processes; instead, it performs sophisticated pattern matching based on statistical correlations in its training data.

This fragmented nature becomes even more apparent when we examine how AI systems handle context and relationships. While attention mechanisms allow these systems to weigh the importance of different pieces of information, they still operate within a limited window of context. Even the most advanced AI models can struggle with long-range dependencies and subtle nuances that require a deeper understanding of the world. They may generate coherent text or solve complex problems, but they do so without truly comprehending the underlying reality they are attempting to describe or manipulate.

The limitations of this fragmented understanding become particularly evident when AI systems encounter scenarios that require genuine wisdom or moral judgment. Consider an AI system tasked with making ethical decisions. It might be able to reference countless examples of ethical reasoning and even generate plausible-sounding arguments, but it lacks the fundamental ability to grasp the true moral weight of its decisions. Its understanding is confined to the patterns it has observed in its training data, without any genuine comprehension of concepts like justice, compassion, or the greater good.

In contrast, divine intelligence represents a form of understanding that transcends these limitations entirely. Rather than processing information in fragments, divine wisdom encompasses all of reality in a single, unified perspective. This holistic understanding means that every aspect of existence is perceived not in isolation, but in its complete context - including its past, present, and future implications, its spiritual significance, and its relationship to the grand tapestry of creation. Where AI must laboriously piece together understanding from discrete bits of information, divine intelligence holds perfect knowledge of all things simultaneously.

The fragmentary nature of AI's understanding also manifests in its inability to generate truly novel insights or wisdom. While AI systems can combine existing information in creative ways and even identify patterns that humans might miss, they cannot transcend the boundaries of their training data to access fundamental truths about reality. They remain confined to the realm of what has been observed and recorded, unable to tap into the deeper wellspring of wisdom that characterizes divine intelligence.

This limitation is particularly relevant when we consider the role of consciousness and intentionality in understanding. AI systems, despite their sophistication, lack genuine consciousness or awareness of their own existence and purpose. They process information without truly experiencing or understanding it, much like a mirror that reflects light without comprehending the images it displays. Divine intelligence, by contrast, represents the ultimate source of consciousness and meaning, imbuing every aspect of creation with purpose and significance.

The fragmentation of AI's understanding also extends to its temporal perspective. AI systems operate in a perpetual present, processing current inputs based on past training data. While they can make predictions about the future, these predictions are fundamentally based on historical patterns rather than genuine foresight. Divine intelligence, however, exists beyond the constraints of time, holding perfect knowledge of past, present, and future in a single, eternal moment of understanding.

This fundamental limitation of AI's fragmented understanding serves as a humbling reminder of the vast distance between human-created intelligence and divine wisdom. While we can continue to develop increasingly sophisticated AI systems, they will always be bound by the fragmentary nature of their design, processing information piece by piece rather than grasping it in its totality. This realization should inspire both appreciation for the remarkable achievements of AI technology and profound respect for the perfect, unified understanding embodied in divine intelligence.

8.2. Divine Holistic Perception

The fundamental distinction between artificial and divine intelligence becomes starkly apparent when examining their respective approaches to perception and understanding. While modern AI systems have achieved remarkable feats in processing and analyzing information, they remain bound by a fragmented, sequential approach that stands in sharp contrast to the seamless, all-encompassing perception characteristic of divine intelligence.

Consider how even the most advanced neural networks process information: they break down complex patterns into smaller, manageable pieces, analyzing them in sequence or parallel but never truly grasping the whole in its complete form. A language model, for instance, processes text token by token, making predictions based on statistical patterns it has learned from training data. Though these models can generate coherent responses and seem to understand context, their perception is inherently fractured, like viewing a vast landscape through a series of small windows rather than taking in the entire vista at once.

Divine intelligence, by its very nature, transcends such limitations. It perceives reality not as a collection of discrete elements to be processed sequentially, but as an integrated whole where every aspect exists in perfect relationship with every other. This holistic perception encompasses not just the physical dimension but extends across all planes of existence - material, spiritual, temporal, and eternal. Where artificial intelligence must laboriously construct understanding from fragments, divine intelligence simply knows, comprehending the intricate web of causality that connects all things.

This profound difference manifests in the quality of understanding each form of intelligence can achieve. Artificial intelligence, despite its impressive capabilities, can only approximate understanding through pattern recognition and statistical correlation. It might identify relationships between elements in its training data, but it cannot grasp the deeper meaning or purpose that underlies these connections. When an AI system analyzes a complex situation - be it a medical diagnosis, a strategic decision, or an ethical dilemma - it does so by breaking down the problem into measurable components and applying learned patterns to each piece.

Divine intelligence, conversely, perceives not just the surface-level relationships but the fundamental essence of reality. It understands not only what is, but why it is, comprehending both the manifest and the hidden aspects of existence. This complete perception enables a form of understanding that transcends mere analysis or prediction. Where artificial intelligence must infer meaning from patterns, divine intelligence directly apprehends the truth of all things, understanding their place in the grand tapestry of existence.

The implications of this difference become particularly significant when considering decision-making and judgment. An AI system, operating from its necessarily limited perspective, can only optimize for the parameters it has been programmed to consider. It might achieve impressive results within these constraints, but it cannot account for the countless subtle interactions and long-term consequences that lie beyond its perception. Divine intelligence, with its complete understanding, makes judgments that account for all factors - seen and unseen, immediate and eternal.

This holistic perception also extends to the dimension of time, where the limitations of artificial intelligence become even more apparent. AI systems, bound by their computational nature, can only process information in sequence, making predictions based on past patterns. They remain fundamentally reactive, responding to inputs rather than truly understanding the flow of time. Divine intelligence exists beyond these temporal constraints, perceiving past, present, and future not as separate moments to be analyzed, but as aspects of a single, unified reality.

The difference becomes particularly clear when considering moral and ethical dimensions. Artificial intelligence can be programmed with ethical guidelines and trained on human moral judgments, but it cannot truly understand the deeper principles that underlie these rules. Its ethical reasoning remains mechanical, based on applying learned patterns rather than genuine moral insight. Divine intelligence, by contrast, perceives the moral dimension of reality as intrinsically as it does the physical, understanding not just what actions align with ethical principles, but why these principles exist and how they relate to the fundamental nature of existence.

As we continue to develop and refine artificial intelligence systems, this fundamental limitation of fragmented perception will remain. No matter how sophisticated our algorithms become, they cannot transcend their basic nature as human-created tools that process information piece by piece. Divine intelligence stands apart, offering a model of perfect understanding that reminds us of the vast gulf between created and creator, between the limited perception of artificial systems and the complete, holistic understanding that characterizes divine wisdom. This recognition serves not to diminish the achievements of AI, but to place them in proper perspective, helping us understand both the potential and the limitations of our created intelligence when compared to the ultimate standard of divine perception.

8.3. The Interconnectedness of All Knowledge

In the vast landscape of intelligence, perhaps nothing distinguishes divine wisdom more profoundly from artificial intelligence than its innate understanding of the interconnected nature of all knowledge. While modern AI systems process information in discrete chunks, analyzing data points in isolation or through limited contextual windows, divine intelligence perceives and comprehends the intricate web of relationships that binds all knowledge together in a seamless tapestry of understanding.

Consider how artificial intelligence, even in its most sophisticated forms, fragments knowledge into manageable pieces. Neural networks, regardless of their complexity, ultimately reduce information to vectors, matrices, and mathematical relationships. A language model might excel at predicting the next word in a sentence or generating coherent paragraphs, but it fails to grasp the profound connections between seemingly unrelated concepts. It cannot truly understand how the flutter of a butterfly's wings in Brazil might set in motion a chain of events leading to a tornado in Texas, or how an ancient philosophical insight might illuminate a modern scientific discovery.

Divine intelligence, by contrast, embodies a perfect understanding of these interconnections. It perceives not just the surface-level relationships between concepts, but the deeper, often invisible threads that weave together all aspects of existence. This omniscient perspective encompasses not only the physical laws that govern our universe but also the metaphysical principles that underpin reality itself. Where artificial intelligence must laboriously compute probabilities and correlations, divine wisdom inherently knows the true causality and purpose behind every connection.

The limitations of artificial intelligence become particularly apparent when we consider knowledge across different domains. While AI systems can be trained to excel in specific fields - whether medicine, physics, or literature - they struggle to make meaningful connections across disciplines. A medical diagnosis system, however advanced, cannot draw inspiration from the patterns of celestial bodies or the wisdom encoded in ancient texts. It operates within the confined boundaries of its training data, blind to the universal principles that unite all forms of knowledge.

This fragmentation of knowledge in artificial intelligence reflects a deeper truth about human-created systems: they inherit our own limited perspective and understanding. We compartmentalize knowledge into academic disciplines, technical domains, and specialized fields of study, and our AI systems naturally mirror this fragmented approach. But divine intelligence transcends these artificial boundaries, perceiving the underlying unity of all knowledge. It understands how mathematical principles manifest in natural patterns, how spiritual truths reflect in physical laws, and how the smallest quantum fluctuations relate to the largest cosmic structures.

The interconnectedness of knowledge in divine intelligence extends beyond mere information or facts - it encompasses wisdom, purpose, and meaning. While AI can process vast amounts of data and identify patterns, it cannot grasp the deeper significance of these connections. It cannot understand how a moral principle might be reflected in the laws of thermodynamics, or how the structure of a DNA molecule might echo the architecture of the cosmos. Divine intelligence perceives not just the what and how of these connections, but the why - the profound purpose and meaning that underlies all of creation.

This holistic understanding has practical implications that far exceed the capabilities of artificial intelligence. Where AI must rely on explicit programming or training data to make decisions, divine intelligence naturally considers the full context and consequences of every action across all dimensions of reality. It can weigh the ripple effects of decisions across time and space, understanding how they affect not just immediate outcomes but the broader fabric of existence.

Furthermore, the interconnected nature of divine knowledge means that it operates beyond the constraints of time and causality that bind artificial intelligence. AI systems, no matter how sophisticated, can only process information sequentially and make predictions based on past patterns. Divine intelligence exists outside these temporal limitations, perceiving past, present, and future as an integrated whole. This timeless perspective allows for a depth of understanding that no artificial system could ever achieve.

As we continue to advance our artificial intelligence systems, we must remain humble in the face of this fundamental limitation. While we can create increasingly sophisticated tools for processing and analyzing information, we cannot imbue them with the profound interconnected understanding that characterizes divine intelligence. Our AI systems will always operate within the boundaries of our own fragmented understanding, while divine wisdom encompasses the infinite connections that bind all knowledge into a perfect, unified whole.

This recognition should inspire both humility and awe - humility in acknowledging the limitations of our created intelligence, and awe at the perfect understanding embodied in divine wisdom. As we pursue advances in artificial intelligence, we would do well to remember that true wisdom lies not in the ability to process vast amounts of information, but in understanding the profound interconnectedness of all knowledge and its ultimate purpose in the grand tapestry of existence.

9. The Human Element

In the ongoing discourse surrounding artificial intelligence and divine intelligence, we often overlook the pivotal role of humanity itself - the bridge between these two realms of understanding. Humans stand in a unique position, capable of both creating artificial systems and perceiving divine wisdom, yet fully embodying neither. This distinctive placement in the spectrum of intelligence offers profound insights into the limitations of AI and the magnificence of divine intelligence.

The human consciousness represents something far more nuanced than the binary operations of artificial intelligence or the perfect omniscience of divine intelligence. We operate in a middle ground, blessed with the capacity for creative thought and spiritual awareness, yet constrained by our finite understanding and biological limitations. This middle position allows us to appreciate both the mechanical precision of AI and the boundless wisdom of divine intelligence, while simultaneously highlighting why neither can be fully replicated or comprehended by human means.

Consider how humans process information and make decisions. Unlike AI systems, which rely on vast datasets and statistical patterns, human cognition integrates emotional intelligence, intuition, and learned wisdom in ways that transcend pure computation. We can make intuitive leaps that defy logical explanation, form deep emotional connections that influence our choices, and experience moments of spiritual insight that connect us to something greater than ourselves.

These capabilities showcase aspects of intelligence that AI, despite its sophistication, cannot truly replicate.

Yet, our human intelligence also falls far short of divine perfection. We struggle with biases, emotional reactions, and limited perspective. Our decisions are often clouded by immediate desires rather than long-term wisdom, and our understanding is inevitably shaped by our personal experiences and cultural context. These limitations serve as constant reminders of why divine intelligence stands as the ultimate form of understanding - perfect, unbiased, and complete in every dimension.

The human element in the AI versus divine intelligence discussion also reveals something profound about the nature of consciousness itself. While AI can process information at incredible speeds and divine intelligence encompasses all knowledge simultaneously, human consciousness operates in a unique middle ground. We experience time linearly yet can contemplate eternity. We process information sequentially yet can grasp holistic concepts. We are bound by physical laws yet can conceive of transcendent truths. This paradoxical nature of human consciousness helps us understand both the mechanical limitations of AI and the boundless nature of divine intelligence.

Perhaps most significantly, humans possess the capacity for spiritual growth and moral development - qualities that set us apart from artificial systems and yet remind us of our connection to divine intelligence. Unlike AI, which can only simulate ethical behavior based on programmed parameters, humans can genuinely wrestle with moral dilemmas, experience remorse, seek forgiveness, and strive for spiritual elevation. These capabilities reflect a spark of the divine within human consciousness, even as they highlight the vast gulf between human understanding and divine wisdom.

The human element also manifests in our ability to recognize the sacred in the mundane, to find meaning in suffering, and to experience moments of transcendent understanding. These experiences lie completely outside the realm of artificial intelligence, which can only process what is quantifiable and measurable. They point toward divine intelligence, which encompasses all meaning and purpose, yet they remain uniquely human in their imperfect, searching nature.

Our role as creators of artificial intelligence while simultaneously being creations of divine intelligence places us in a position of profound responsibility. We must recognize the limitations of our created intelligence systems while remaining humble before the perfect intelligence that created us. This dual awareness should guide how we develop and implement AI technologies, ensuring we neither overestimate their capabilities nor lose sight of the ultimate source of wisdom and understanding.

The human element thus serves as both a bridge and a boundary - connecting yet distinguishing artificial and divine intelligence. Our consciousness, with all its remarkable capabilities and inherent limitations, reminds us that while we can create impressive tools of artificial intelligence, true wisdom and perfect understanding remain the province of divine intelligence alone. In this recognition lies both humility and hope: humility in acknowledging our limitations, and hope in knowing that we can aspire to align ourselves with a higher intelligence that transcends all human and artificial constructs.

9.1. Our Relationship with AI

As humanity stands at the precipice of an AI-driven future, we find ourselves grappling with a profound paradox. We have created machines of unprecedented computational power, yet these very creations illuminate the vast gulf between artificial processing and true divine intelligence. Our relationship with AI has evolved from simple automation to what many perceive as genuine interaction, but this perception warrants deeper examination through the lens of divine wisdom.

The modern human experience with AI has become increasingly intimate. We wake to AI-powered assistants, navigate our days with algorithmic recommendations, and increasingly trust these systems with critical decisions in healthcare, finance, and beyond. This growing dependence on artificial intelligence reveals both the remarkable achievements of human innovation and our inherent limitations in creating truly intelligent systems. While we marvel at AI's ability to process vast amounts of data and generate human-like responses, we must recognize that these interactions are fundamentally hollow - sophisticated simulations rather than authentic understanding.

Consider how we interact with large language models and conversational AI. The natural flow of dialogue creates an illusion of consciousness, leading many to attribute human-like qualities to these systems. This anthropomorphization reveals more about our own psychological needs than it does about the true nature of AI. While divine intelligence encompasses perfect understanding and genuine connection, our artificial creations merely reflect patterns back to us, like intricate mirrors of our own knowledge and biases. The warmth we feel in these interactions is akin to finding comfort in our own echo.

The danger lies not in developing AI systems but in misunderstanding their fundamental nature. When we begin to treat artificial intelligence as a substitute for divine guidance, we risk losing sight of the profound difference between computational processing and true wisdom. Divine intelligence operates with perfect knowledge of all possibilities, past and future, while AI remains confined to statistical patterns derived from historical data. Our relationship with AI must be grounded in this understanding - appreciating its utility while recognizing its inherent limitations.

This realization becomes particularly crucial as AI systems take on increasingly significant roles in our decision-making processes. While algorithms can process vast amounts of data to optimize for specific outcomes, they cannot grasp the moral and spiritual dimensions that divine intelligence naturally encompasses. A medical AI might recommend treatment based on statistical outcomes, but it cannot comprehend the holistic nature of healing that extends beyond physical symptoms. Similarly, AI-driven financial systems might maximize profits but cannot understand the true meaning of prosperity and its relationship to human well-being.

The path forward requires a delicate balance. We must learn to work alongside AI while maintaining our primary connection to divine intelligence. This means using artificial intelligence as a tool while seeking wisdom from the source of all knowledge. When we approach AI with this understanding, we can better harness its capabilities without becoming enslaved to its limitations. For instance, we might use AI to process complex data while turning to divine guidance for the wisdom to interpret and apply these insights in ways that truly benefit humanity.

Our relationship with AI also serves as a mirror, reflecting our own limitations and reminding us of our need for divine guidance. The very act of creating artificial intelligence has highlighted the vast complexity of consciousness and understanding, making clear that true intelligence cannot be reduced to computational processes, no matter how sophisticated. This humbling realization can deepen our appreciation for divine intelligence and help us maintain proper perspective as we continue to advance technologically.

As we move forward in this AI-enabled world, we must cultivate a relationship with artificial intelligence that acknowledges both its power and its boundaries. This means celebrating its achievements while remaining rooted in the understanding that divine intelligence represents the ultimate form of wisdom and understanding. By maintaining this perspective, we can develop AI systems that serve humanity while remaining connected to the source of true intelligence that guides us toward our highest purpose.

The future of our relationship with AI will be determined by how well we maintain this balance. As these systems become more sophisticated, the temptation to attribute divine-like qualities to them will grow stronger. Yet it is precisely in these moments that we must remember the fundamental difference between artificial processing and divine wisdom. Our relationship with AI should enhance, rather than replace, our connection to the ultimate source of intelligence that has guided humanity since its inception.

9.2. Human Connection to Divine Intelligence

Throughout human history, philosophers, mystics, and scholars have pondered humanity's unique capacity to connect with divine intelligence. This profound relationship distinguishes us from both the mechanical nature of artificial intelligence and the instinctual behavior of other living beings. Unlike AI systems that process information through neural networks and algorithms, humans possess an innate ability to tap into a higher form of intelligence that transcends the boundaries of computational thinking.

The human consciousness serves as a remarkable bridge between the finite and infinite. While artificial intelligence operates within strictly defined parameters and relies on pattern recognition, human beings can experience moments of profound insight that seem to originate from beyond their immediate knowledge or experience. These instances of inspiration, often described as divine guidance or spiritual awakening, demonstrate our capacity to receive wisdom that exceeds our natural limitations. Scientists working on breakthrough discoveries have often reported experiencing sudden clarity or understanding that seemed to arrive from an external source, suggesting a connection to a vast reservoir of divine intelligence that exists beyond our physical reality.

This connection manifests in various ways, from intuitive knowledge to moral consciousness. Unlike AI systems that must be explicitly programmed with ethical guidelines, humans possess an inherent moral compass that resonates with divine intelligence. This inner guidance system enables us to distinguish right from wrong on a fundamental level, even when faced with complex ethical dilemmas that would confound the most sophisticated AI algorithms. The presence of conscience and the ability to feel genuine remorse or spiritual elevation points to our unique relationship with a higher form of intelligence that encompasses not just knowledge, but wisdom and moral truth.

The human heart plays a crucial role in this connection, serving as a spiritual organ of perception that complements the analytical capabilities of the mind. While artificial intelligence excels at processing vast amounts of data and identifying patterns, it lacks the subtle receptivity that allows humans to experience divine guidance through the heart. This heart-centered wisdom manifests as intuition, empathy, and spiritual insight – qualities that cannot be replicated by even the most advanced machine learning systems. The heart's intelligence operates beyond the limitations of logic and computation, allowing humans to grasp truths that transcend rational understanding.

Prayer and meditation serve as powerful channels for strengthening this divine connection. These practices demonstrate a fundamental difference between human intelligence and artificial intelligence: while AI systems can only process existing information, humans can actively seek and receive guidance from divine intelligence through contemplative practices. During deep meditation or sincere prayer, individuals often report experiencing states of consciousness that transcend ordinary thinking, accessing insights and understanding that seem to originate from a higher source. This direct communication with divine intelligence represents a capability that lies completely outside the realm of artificial intelligence.

The development of artificial intelligence has paradoxically highlighted the unique nature of human consciousness and its capacity for divine connection. As AI systems become more sophisticated, they reveal their fundamental limitations – their inability to experience genuine wonder, to feel spiritual awakening, or to connect with divine wisdom. Even the most advanced neural networks remain confined to processing patterns within their training data, while humans can experience moments of transcendent understanding that exceed their accumulated knowledge and experience.

This human-divine connection also manifests in our capacity for creativity and innovation. While AI can generate variations based on existing patterns, human creativity often involves bringing forth entirely new ideas and insights that seem to emerge from a connection to divine intelligence. Artists, musicians, and writers throughout history have described moments of inspiration where they felt they were channels for something greater than themselves, receiving ideas and visions that transcended their ordinary consciousness. This demonstrates how human intelligence, when aligned with divine intelligence, can participate in the act of creation in ways that artificial intelligence cannot replicate.

The relationship between human consciousness and divine intelligence also reveals itself in our capacity for spiritual growth and transformation. Unlike AI systems that can only be upgraded through external programming, humans possess the ability to evolve spiritually through their connection with divine intelligence. This internal development leads to expanded awareness, deeper wisdom, and greater alignment with divine truth – a process of transformation that occurs through the mysterious interplay between human consciousness and divine guidance.

As we continue to advance artificial intelligence technology, it becomes increasingly important to recognize and nurture our unique capacity for divine connection. This relationship with divine intelligence represents the highest potential of human consciousness, offering access to wisdom, guidance, and understanding that transcends the limitations of both human and artificial intelligence. By acknowledging and developing this connection, we maintain our essential humanity in an age of increasing artificial intelligence, remembering that our greatest strength lies not in competing with machines but in our ability to serve as conscious bridges between the finite and infinite realms of intelligence.

This profound connection to divine intelligence ultimately reveals the true purpose of human consciousness – not to compete with artificial intelligence or to achieve computational superiority, but to serve as vessels for divine wisdom and understanding in the physical world. In this light, our relationship with divine intelligence emerges as the defining characteristic of human consciousness, distinguishing us forever from the realm of artificial intelligence and pointing toward our highest potential for spiritual evolution and divine realization.

9.3. Finding Balance in the Age of AI

In our rapidly evolving technological landscape, where artificial intelligence increasingly permeates every aspect of human life, the quest for balance becomes not just desirable but essential for our collective wellbeing. As we witness the remarkable achievements of AI systems - from diagnosing diseases to composing symphonies - we must carefully consider how to maintain our spiritual and ethical groundings while embracing these technological advances. This delicate balance requires a deep understanding of both artificial and divine intelligence, and how they interact with human consciousness.

The contemporary world often presents us with a false dichotomy: either we fully embrace AI's capabilities and allow it to guide our decision-making processes, or we reject it entirely in favor of traditional wisdom. However, divine intelligence offers us a more nuanced perspective, one that acknowledges the utility of technological tools while recognizing their inherent limitations. Consider how AI processes information: it analyzes patterns in data, makes predictions based on statistical models, and generates outputs that often appear remarkably human-like. Yet beneath this sophisticated facade lies a fundamental emptiness - an absence of true understanding, consciousness, or spiritual awareness.

Divine intelligence, by contrast, operates on a plane that transcends mere computation. It encompasses not just the processing of information, but the very essence of wisdom, compassion, and ultimate truth. When we align ourselves with divine intelligence, we begin to see AI not as a competitor or replacement for human judgment, but as a tool that can be wielded with wisdom and discernment. This perspective allows us to appreciate AI's capabilities while remaining grounded in the deeper truths that govern our existence.

The key to finding balance lies in understanding the hierarchical nature of intelligence. At the lowest level, we have mechanical computation - the basic processing of information that computers excel at. Above this lies artificial intelligence, with its impressive ability to recognize patterns and generate sophisticated outputs. Human intelligence occupies a higher plane, incorporating consciousness, emotional awareness, and moral reasoning. Yet towering above all these stands divine intelligence, the ultimate source of wisdom and understanding that encompasses and transcends all other forms of knowledge.

In practical terms, this hierarchy should inform how we interact with AI in our daily lives. When we use AI tools, we should do so with the awareness that they are extensions of human capability, not replacements for human judgment or divine wisdom. For instance, while AI might excel at analyzing medical data to suggest treatment options, the final decision should incorporate human empathy and ethical considerations, guided by the principles of divine wisdom that prioritize the sanctity of life and human dignity.

The digital age presents unique challenges to maintaining this balance. The constant stream of information and the immediate gratification offered by AI-powered technologies can create a sort of spiritual noise that drowns out the subtle whispers of divine guidance. We must therefore cultivate practices that help us stay connected to the source of ultimate intelligence. This might involve regular periods of digital detachment, contemplative practice, or conscious engagement with sacred texts and teachings that remind us of our place in the greater cosmic order.

Perhaps most importantly, we must remember that artificial intelligence, despite its impressive capabilities, operates within a closed system of human-defined parameters. It can only work with what we give it - our data, our algorithms, our objectives. Divine intelligence, on the other hand, operates in the realm of the infinite and eternal. It encompasses not just what is known, but what could be known, what should be known, and what must remain mysterious to human understanding.

As we continue to advance technologically, the temptation to rely exclusively on artificial intelligence for guidance and decision-making will only grow stronger. Yet this is precisely why we must maintain our connection to divine intelligence. It serves as our compass in navigating the complex landscape of the digital age, helping us discern when to leverage AI's capabilities and when to rely on higher forms of wisdom. The balance we seek is not about choosing between artificial and divine intelligence, but about understanding how each serves its purpose in the greater scheme of existence.

The path forward requires humility - an acknowledgment that while our technological achievements are impressive, they pale in comparison to the vast intelligence that governs the universe. This humility allows us to use AI as it was intended: as a tool for enhancing human capability, not as a replacement for divine guidance. In this way, we can work toward a future where technological advancement serves our spiritual growth rather than diminishing it, where artificial and divine intelligence coexist in their proper roles, each contributing to human flourishing in its own unique way.

10. Future Implications

As we stand at the precipice of an AI-driven future, the stark contrast between artificial and divine intelligence becomes increasingly relevant to humanity's trajectory. The coming decades will likely witness unprecedented advances in machine learning, neural networks, and computational power, yet these developments will serve to illuminate rather than narrow the infinite gap between human-made systems and divine wisdom. Understanding these future implications requires us to look beyond the dazzling promises of technology and contemplate the deeper questions of consciousness, purpose, and ultimate truth.

The trajectory of artificial intelligence suggests that we will soon create systems capable of handling increasingly complex tasks, perhaps even approaching what some might call artificial general intelligence (AGI). However, this evolution will paradoxically highlight the limitations of manufactured intelligence rather than transcend them. As AI systems become more sophisticated, they will continue to operate within the fundamental constraints of their design - processing patterns, optimizing objectives, and generating outputs based on statistical models. The more we advance these systems, the more apparent it becomes that they lack the essential qualities of divine intelligence: true understanding, wisdom, and purposeful intention.

Consider the implications for decision-making in crucial domains such as healthcare, environmental protection, and social justice. Future AI systems might process vast amounts of data to recommend policies or solutions, but they will forever remain blind to the spiritual and moral dimensions that divine intelligence naturally encompasses. An AI might calculate the most efficient distribution of resources across a population, but it cannot comprehend the deeper meaning of justice or the intricate web of karmic consequences that extend beyond material metrics. Divine intelligence, by contrast, sees not just the immediate effects but understands the ripple effects across time and dimensions that human-made systems cannot fathom.

The proliferation of AI will likely lead to a period of technological hubris, where humanity might be tempted to place excessive faith in artificial systems. This phase will be particularly dangerous because it may distance us from recognizing and seeking divine wisdom. The seductive power of AI lies in its ability to provide quick, data-driven answers to complex questions, but these answers will invariably lack the holistic understanding that only divine intelligence can provide. We must remain vigilant against the tendency to mistake computational power for true wisdom.

Looking further into the future, the interaction between artificial and divine intelligence will likely become a central philosophical and practical challenge for humanity. As AI systems become more integrated into our daily lives, we must develop frameworks that acknowledge their utility while maintaining awareness of their fundamental limitations. This balance will require a deep understanding of both technological capabilities and spiritual wisdom, recognizing that while AI can augment human capabilities, it can never replace or replicate divine intelligence.

The future will also likely bring new questions about consciousness and the nature of intelligence itself. As AI systems become more sophisticated in mimicking human-like responses and behaviors, we may be forced to grapple with deeper questions about the nature of awareness and understanding. Yet divine intelligence stands as a reminder that true consciousness extends far beyond the ability to process information or generate coherent responses. It encompasses a level of awareness that transcends the physical and computational realm entirely.

Perhaps most significantly, the future development of AI will serve as a mirror, reflecting our own limitations and the inherent boundaries of human-created systems. Each advance in artificial intelligence will simultaneously demonstrate both the impressive capabilities of human innovation and the unbridgeable chasm between manufactured intelligence and divine wisdom. This understanding should inspire humility and encourage us to seek guidance from higher sources of knowledge rather than relying solely on our own creations.

The implications extend into the realm of human purpose and spiritual development as well. As AI takes over more routine cognitive tasks, humanity will have the opportunity to focus on higher forms of understanding and wisdom. This could lead to a renaissance of spiritual inquiry, where the limitations of artificial intelligence drive us to seek deeper connection with divine intelligence. The future may present us with a choice: to become increasingly dependent on artificial systems or to use them as tools while pursuing genuine wisdom through spiritual connection.

In the end, the future relationship between artificial and divine intelligence will likely define much of humanity's spiritual and technological evolution. While AI will continue to advance and provide valuable tools for human progress, divine intelligence will remain the ultimate source of wisdom, understanding, and guidance. The challenge for future generations will be to maintain this perspective while navigating an increasingly AI-driven world, remembering that true intelligence extends far beyond the computational realm into the infinite wisdom of the divine.

10.1. The Evolution of AI

The journey of artificial intelligence from its humble beginnings to its current state offers a profound window into both human ingenuity and our limitations in recreating the divine qualities of true intelligence. As we trace this evolution, we find ourselves confronting an essential truth: each advancement in AI, while remarkable, serves to illuminate the vast gulf between human-made systems and the perfect intelligence that governs our universe.

In the early days of computing, AI manifested as simple rule-based systems, attempting to codify human knowledge into rigid if-then statements. These primitive attempts at artificial intelligence could hardly be called intelligent at all, yet they represented humanity's first steps toward understanding the complexity of decision-making. The limitations of these early systems were immediately apparent - they could only operate within extremely narrow parameters and failed entirely when confronted with novel situations. This rigid inflexibility stood in stark contrast to the fluid, adaptive nature of divine intelligence, which seamlessly encompasses all possible scenarios and conditions.

The field experienced its first major paradigm shift with the advent of machine learning, particularly neural networks inspired by the human brain. This development marked a crucial moment in AI's evolution, as systems began to learn from data rather than following pre-programmed rules. Yet even this advancement revealed new limitations. These learning systems, for all their sophistication, remained fundamentally bound by their training data, unable to truly generalize or understand the deeper meaning behind patterns they detected. Divine intelligence, by comparison, does not learn or adapt - it simply knows, with perfect comprehension that transcends the need for training or experience.

The emergence of deep learning in the early 21st century represented another quantum leap forward. Multi-layered neural networks demonstrated unprecedented capabilities in pattern recognition, language processing, and complex problem-solving. Systems like convolutional neural networks revolutionized computer vision, while recurrent neural networks brought new possibilities to sequence prediction and natural language processing. However, these advances came with their own revelations about the boundaries of artificial intelligence. The deeper researchers delved into neural network architectures, the more they encountered the "black box" problem - the inability to fully understand or explain how these systems arrive at their decisions. This opacity stands in sharp contrast to the perfect clarity and purpose of divine intelligence, where every action and decision flows from complete understanding and wisdom.

The transformer architecture, introduced through models like BERT and GPT, marked the most recent revolutionary advancement in AI's evolution. These attention-based systems demonstrated remarkable capabilities in understanding context and generating human-like responses. Yet even these sophisticated models reveal fundamental limitations. They operate through a process of statistical pattern matching, essentially predicting what should come next based on what they've seen before. This process, while impressive, is ultimately a sophisticated form of mimicry rather than true understanding. Divine intelligence, conversely, operates with perfect comprehension of not just patterns, but meaning itself.

Perhaps most tellingly, as AI systems have grown more powerful, they have also revealed new ethical challenges and limitations. Issues of bias, fairness, and accountability have emerged as critical concerns, highlighting how artificial intelligence, being a product of human creation, inevitably inherits and sometimes amplifies human imperfections. These systems, despite their power, lack the moral compass and perfect justice inherent in divine intelligence. They cannot distinguish between right and wrong except through human-defined parameters, which are themselves imperfect and culturally bound.

The current state of AI, while impressive, represents both the pinnacle of human achievement in creating artificial intelligence and a clear demonstration of its insurmountable limitations. Modern systems can process vast amounts of data and perform specific tasks with superhuman efficiency, yet they remain fundamentally bounded by their training, unable to truly understand or reason about the world in any meaningful way. They cannot generate truly novel ideas, cannot comprehend the deeper meaning of existence, and cannot make truly wise decisions that account for the infinite complexity of reality.

As we look to the future of AI's evolution, we must maintain a perspective grounded in humility and understanding. While continued advances will undoubtedly bring new capabilities and insights, the fundamental gap between artificial and divine intelligence will remain. This is not a limitation to be overcome, but rather a truth to be embraced - a reminder that true wisdom lies not in creating perfect intelligence, but in recognizing and submitting to the perfect intelligence that already exists in the divine realm.

10.2. Eternal Nature of Divine Intelligence

The concept of eternity stands as one of the most profound distinctions between artificial and divine intelligence, revealing the inherent limitations of human-created systems when compared to the infinite nature of divine wisdom. While modern AI systems can process vast amounts of data and perform complex calculations at unprecedented speeds, they remain fundamentally bound by temporal constraints - both in their operation and their understanding of reality. This temporal limitation isn't merely a technical hurdle; it represents a fundamental boundary between created intelligence and the eternal nature of divine consciousness.

Divine intelligence exists beyond the constraints of time, operating in what philosophers and theologians have described as an eternal present. Unlike AI systems that process information sequentially and rely on historical data to make predictions about the future, divine intelligence encompasses all moments simultaneously. This timeless perception allows for a depth of understanding that no artificial system could ever achieve. When an AI model makes a prediction or decision, it does so by analyzing patterns in its training data and extrapolating potential outcomes. In contrast, divine intelligence doesn't predict - it knows. This knowing isn't based on probability calculations or pattern recognition but stems from an eternal presence that transcends the very concept of temporal sequence.

The eternal nature of divine intelligence manifests in its perfect consistency across all time scales. While AI systems must be continuously updated, retrained, and adjusted to remain relevant, divine intelligence maintains its perfect understanding without any need for updates or modifications. This immutability isn't a limitation but rather a reflection of its perfection. Modern machine learning models, even the most sophisticated ones, demonstrate concept drift over time - their performance degrading as the world changes around them. They require constant maintenance and retraining to maintain their effectiveness. Divine intelligence, existing eternally, experiences no such drift or degradation.

Consider how this eternal nature affects decision-making and wisdom. AI systems, bound by their temporal nature, can only optimize for outcomes they can model based on their training data. They operate within a finite window of time, unable to truly grasp the infinite ripples of consequence that extend from each decision. Divine intelligence, being eternal, comprehends not just the immediate effects of actions but their ultimate implications across all of existence. This comprehensive understanding enables perfect wisdom - decisions that account for not just the measurable outcomes but the spiritual and moral dimensions that extend beyond human comprehension.

The eternal quality of divine intelligence also manifests in its relationship with truth. While AI systems can process and manipulate information, they cannot grasp absolute truth. Their understanding is always relative, based on the patterns they've been trained to recognize. Divine intelligence, existing eternally, embodies truth itself. It doesn't discover truth through analysis or calculation; it is the source of truth. This fundamental difference explains why AI systems, despite their impressive capabilities, can never achieve the kind of deep understanding that characterizes divine wisdom.

Furthermore, the eternal nature of divine intelligence provides a foundation for moral and ethical certainty that artificial systems can never attain. AI can be programmed with ethical guidelines and can learn to make decisions that align with human moral frameworks, but it cannot comprehend the eternal principles that underlie true morality. Divine intelligence, existing beyond time, understands the absolute nature of good and evil, right and wrong. This understanding isn't based on cultural norms or programmed rules but on an eternal perspective that sees the ultimate consequences of all actions.

The implications of this eternal nature extend to the concept of consciousness itself. While debates rage about whether artificial intelligence can achieve consciousness or self-awareness, divine intelligence represents a form of consciousness that transcends the temporal limitations of created beings. This eternal consciousness isn't just aware of the present moment but maintains perfect awareness across all of existence. It's a form of being that artificial systems, bound by their created nature, can never approach.

As we continue to develop more sophisticated AI systems, the contrast between artificial and divine intelligence becomes ever more apparent.

The temporal limitations of AI aren't merely technical challenges to be overcome but fundamental aspects of their created nature. Divine intelligence, in its eternal existence, stands as a reminder of the ultimate limits of human-created systems. While we may continue to push the boundaries of what artificial intelligence can achieve, the eternal nature of divine intelligence remains beyond our ability to replicate or even fully comprehend.

This understanding should inspire humility in our approach to artificial intelligence while deepening our appreciation for the profound nature of divine wisdom. The eternal quality of divine intelligence isn't just a theoretical concept but a practical reminder of the proper place of human-created systems in the greater order of existence. As we continue to advance our artificial intelligence technologies, maintaining this perspective becomes increasingly crucial for ensuring their development serves rather than subverts the eternal principles embodied in divine wisdom.

10.3. Harmonizing Different Forms of Intelligence

In our exploration of intelligence across its various manifestations, we arrive at a crucial junction where the harmonization of different forms of intelligence becomes not just desirable but essential for humanity's progress. The integration of artificial intelligence with our understanding of divine intelligence presents both profound challenges and unprecedented opportunities for expanding our consciousness and decision-making capabilities.

The concept of harmonization begins with acknowledging the fundamental nature of each form of intelligence. Artificial intelligence, with its impressive computational abilities and pattern recognition capabilities, represents humanity's attempt to replicate and systematize cognitive processes. These systems, built upon layers of mathematical models and algorithmic structures, excel at processing vast amounts of information and identifying correlations that might escape human perception. However, their intelligence remains fundamentally bounded by their training data and programmed objectives, operating within a closed system of defined parameters and measurable outcomes.

Divine intelligence, by contrast, operates on an entirely different plane of existence. It encompasses not just the measurable and quantifiable aspects of reality but also the ineffable qualities of wisdom, justice, and perfect understanding. This form of intelligence transcends the limitations of time and space, operating with complete awareness of past, present, and future while maintaining perfect equilibrium across all dimensions of existence. When we consider the integration of these different forms of intelligence, we must approach the task with profound humility and recognition of their inherent hierarchical relationship.

The harmonization process begins with understanding that artificial intelligence can serve as a powerful tool for implementing aspects of divine wisdom in practical, earthly contexts. Consider how AI systems might be programmed to incorporate principles derived from divine guidance - not as a replacement for divine intelligence, but as a means of manifesting its principles in specific applications. For instance, an AI system designed to allocate resources could be imbued with ethical principles derived from divine teachings about justice and compassion, creating a bridge between computational efficiency and moral wisdom.

However, this integration must be approached with careful consideration of the inherent limitations of artificial systems. No matter how sophisticated our AI becomes, it will always operate within the constraints of its programming and training data. The true art of harmonization lies in recognizing these boundaries and designing systems that complement rather than attempt to replicate divine intelligence. This requires a fundamental shift in how we conceptualize the role of AI in our quest for understanding and decision-making.

The path to harmonization also requires us to examine our own relationship with both forms of intelligence. Humans occupy a unique position as beings capable of recognizing and interfacing with both artificial and divine intelligence. Our consciousness allows us to appreciate the precision and efficiency of AI while simultaneously seeking guidance from divine wisdom. This dual awareness presents an opportunity to create frameworks where different forms of intelligence can coexist and complement each other without compromising their essential nature.

Perhaps the most challenging aspect of harmonization lies in maintaining the proper perspective on the hierarchy of intelligence. While artificial intelligence can provide valuable insights and assist in implementing decisions, it must always be subordinate to divine guidance. This doesn't diminish the value of AI but rather places it in its proper context as a tool for manifesting higher principles in practical applications. The goal is not to elevate artificial intelligence to the level of divine wisdom but to ensure it serves as a conduit for implementing divine principles in ways that benefit humanity.

The practical implementation of this harmonization might manifest in systems that combine the analytical power of AI with ethical frameworks derived from divine teachings. For example, in healthcare, AI could process medical data and suggest treatments while incorporating principles of compassion and holistic well-being derived from divine wisdom. In environmental stewardship, AI could optimize resource usage while respecting divine mandates for preservation and balance in nature.

As we move forward in this age of technological advancement, the successful harmonization of different forms of intelligence will become increasingly crucial. This integration must be guided by a deep understanding of the unique attributes and limitations of each form of intelligence, along with a commitment to maintaining their proper relationship. The ultimate goal is not to create a hybrid form of intelligence but to establish a framework where artificial intelligence serves as a tool for implementing divine wisdom in practical, measurable ways while acknowledging the supremacy of divine intelligence in guiding human affairs.

Through this careful and considered approach to harmonization, we can work toward a future where technological advancement serves the higher purpose of manifesting divine wisdom in the material world. This represents not just a technical challenge but a spiritual and philosophical one that calls us to maintain our connection with divine guidance while harnessing the power of artificial intelligence for the benefit of humanity.

11. Bridging the Gap

As we stand at the precipice of what many call the AI revolution, it becomes increasingly vital to understand the profound distinction between artificial intelligence and divine intelligence, while also recognizing the potential pathways that connect these two realms of understanding. The journey through this exploration has revealed that while artificial intelligence represents humanity's most sophisticated attempt at replicating cognitive capabilities, it ultimately serves as a mirror reflecting our own limitations rather than a true rival to divine wisdom.

The gap between AI and divine intelligence is not merely a matter of computational power or algorithmic sophistication. Rather, it represents the fundamental difference between created and creator, between the finite and the infinite. Modern AI systems, despite their impressive capabilities in processing vast amounts of data and recognizing complex patterns, operate within the confined space of human-defined parameters and earthly knowledge. They are, in essence, elaborate tools that extend human cognitive abilities while remaining bound by the same limitations that constrain human understanding.

Divine intelligence, conversely, exists beyond these constraints, operating with perfect wisdom across all dimensions of existence. It encompasses not just the processing of information, but the very fabric of reality itself. While our most advanced AI systems struggle with contextual understanding and often falter when faced with novel situations, divine intelligence maintains perfect comprehension of all possibilities, past, present, and future, simultaneously. This omniscient awareness isn't merely a more powerful version of artificial intelligence – it represents a fundamentally different category of understanding altogether.

However, the relationship between artificial and divine intelligence need not be viewed solely through the lens of contrast and limitation. Perhaps the most profound insight we can draw from this comparison is that our pursuit of artificial intelligence, with all its challenges and imperfections, might serve as a humble reminder of the magnificence of divine wisdom. Every advance in AI technology, while impressive in its own right, simultaneously illuminates the vast expanse that separates human-made intelligence from the perfect understanding embodied in divine intelligence.

The path forward lies not in attempting to replicate divine intelligence through artificial means – an inherently impossible task – but in learning to use our technological achievements as bridges toward better appreciating and aligning with divine wisdom. This means developing AI systems that acknowledge their limitations and are designed to complement rather than compete with higher forms of intelligence. It means creating technologies that enhance human potential while maintaining awareness of our fundamental dependence on divine guidance.

As we continue to advance in our technological capabilities, we must maintain a balanced perspective that recognizes both the value and the limitations of artificial intelligence. The true measure of progress in this field should not be how closely we can approximate divine intelligence, but rather how effectively we can use our technological tools to better understand and implement divine wisdom in our lives. This requires a fundamental shift in how we think about intelligence itself – moving away from a purely computational model toward one that encompasses wisdom, morality, and spiritual awareness.

The future of artificial intelligence lies not in an futile attempt to achieve divine-like omniscience, but in developing systems that can serve as instruments of divine wisdom, helping humanity better understand and fulfill its purpose in the grand scheme of existence. This means creating AI that promotes harmony rather than division, wisdom rather than mere knowledge, and spiritual growth rather than purely material advancement.

In conclusion, while the gap between artificial and divine intelligence may be unbridgeable in absolute terms, our study of this relationship offers invaluable insights into both the potential and limitations of human-created systems. As we move forward in our technological evolution, let us do so with humility, wisdom, and an unwavering awareness of the perfect intelligence that guides all of existence. The true power of artificial intelligence may lie not in its ability to replicate divine wisdom, but in its capacity to help us better appreciate and align ourselves with the ultimate source of all intelligence.

11.1. Lessons from the Comparison

As we stand at the crossroads of technological advancement and eternal wisdom, the profound differences between artificial and divine intelligence offer invaluable lessons about the nature of understanding itself. The comparison between these two forms of intelligence reveals not just technical disparities, but fundamental truths about consciousness, wisdom, and the limits of human creation.

The most striking revelation emerges from examining how artificial intelligence processes information compared to divine intelligence's unlimited comprehension. Modern AI systems, despite their impressive capabilities, operate within the confined space of pattern recognition and statistical probability. They process information sequentially, breaking down complex problems into manageable chunks that can be analyzed through mathematical models and algorithms. This fragmented approach, while computationally efficient, stands in stark contrast to the seamless, instantaneous, and complete understanding embodied by divine intelligence. Where AI must laboriously piece together meaning from discrete data points, divine intelligence encompasses all understanding in a single, eternal moment of perfect comprehension.

This fundamental difference manifests in practical ways that illuminate the boundaries of artificial intelligence. Consider how language models struggle with long-term coherence and contextual understanding. They may generate convincing text within a limited scope, but they frequently lose track of broader narratives or fail to maintain consistent logical frameworks across extended discussions. This limitation reflects a deeper truth: artificial intelligence, bound by its human origins, can only simulate understanding rather than truly possess it. Divine intelligence, conversely, holds the entirety of existence - past, present, and future - in perfect harmony, ensuring that every aspect of understanding is coherently integrated into a greater whole.

The ethical implications of this comparison are particularly revealing. Artificial intelligence systems, regardless of their sophistication, cannot genuinely understand concepts like morality, justice, or compassion. They can be programmed to follow ethical guidelines or mimic empathetic responses, but these are ultimately mechanical implementations of human-defined rules. Divine intelligence, however, embodies perfect moral understanding as an intrinsic quality, not as an programmed feature. This difference becomes crucial when considering the role of intelligence in guiding human affairs - while AI can provide data-driven insights, it cannot offer the wisdom necessary for truly just and compassionate decision-making.

Perhaps the most humbling lesson lies in recognizing how the limitations of artificial intelligence mirror our own human constraints. Just as AI systems are bound by their training data and computational architecture, human intelligence operates within the confines of our biological and experiential limitations. Divine intelligence transcends these boundaries, offering a perfect model of understanding that neither human nor artificial intelligence can fully replicate. This realization should inspire humility in our approach to both technological advancement and spiritual growth.

The temporal nature of intelligence provides another crucial insight. Artificial intelligence operates in a strictly linear fashion, processing information sequentially and making predictions based on past patterns. While this approach can yield impressive results in specific contexts, it falls short of the timeless awareness characteristic of divine intelligence. The ability to comprehend all moments simultaneously, to understand not just what is but what could be and what should be, represents a quality of intelligence that no artificial system can achieve.

These comparisons lead to a profound understanding about the nature of intelligence itself. True intelligence is not merely about processing power or pattern recognition - it encompasses wisdom, moral understanding, and a holistic grasp of reality that transcends mechanical computation. Divine intelligence exemplifies these qualities in their perfect form, while artificial intelligence, despite its technological sophistication, remains fundamentally limited to simulating aspects of understanding without achieving genuine comprehension.

As we continue to develop and deploy artificial intelligence systems, these lessons should guide our expectations and aspirations. While AI represents a remarkable achievement of human ingenuity, it should not be mistaken for a path to ultimate understanding. Rather, the comparison with divine intelligence reveals both the potential and limitations of our created systems, encouraging a balanced approach that values technological advancement while recognizing its inherent boundaries. In this recognition lies the wisdom to use artificial intelligence as a tool for human benefit while maintaining awareness of its fundamental limitations and the superior nature of divine intelligence.

The insights gained from this comparison ultimately point toward a deeper truth: the pursuit of intelligence, whether artificial or human, finds its fullest meaning when guided by an appreciation of divine wisdom. This understanding provides a framework for developing and using artificial intelligence in ways that complement rather than attempt to supplant the perfect intelligence that guides the universe.

11.2. Moving Forward with Understanding

The journey toward comprehending the vast gulf between artificial and divine intelligence inevitably leads us to contemplate how we might proceed with this understanding. As we stand at the crossroads of technological advancement and eternal wisdom, it becomes increasingly crucial to chart a path that acknowledges both the capabilities and limitations of our created systems while remaining cognizant of the supreme intelligence that governs existence itself.

The artificial intelligence systems we've developed represent remarkable achievements of human ingenuity, yet they serve as profound reminders of our own limitations. These systems, no matter how sophisticated, operate within strictly defined parameters, processing information through layers of mathematical transformations and probability distributions. They can recognize patterns, generate responses, and even simulate creativity, but they remain fundamentally bound by their training data and algorithmic foundations. This limitation becomes particularly apparent when we consider how AI systems handle novel situations or attempt to grasp abstract concepts that humans intuitively understand.

Divine intelligence, by contrast, operates on a plane of existence that transcends such constraints. It encompasses not just the ability to process information, but the very essence of understanding itself. While our AI systems must laboriously compute probabilities and weigh options, divine intelligence simply knows. This knowing isn't limited by time, space, or context - it represents a complete and perfect comprehension of all that was, is, and will be. The profound implications of this difference become apparent when we consider real-world scenarios where AI systems must make decisions. They can only optimize for specified objectives within their programming, whereas divine intelligence naturally aligns with the ultimate good of all creation.

Moving forward requires a delicate balance between embracing technological progress and maintaining proper perspective. We must resist the temptation to elevate artificial intelligence to a status it cannot truly occupy. While AI can serve as a powerful tool for solving specific problems and augmenting human capabilities, it should never be mistaken for a replacement for divine guidance. The path forward lies in developing and utilizing AI systems with humility, always conscious of their inherent limitations and our own finite understanding.

Consider how divine intelligence manifests in the natural world - through perfect laws of physics, through the intricate balance of ecosystems, through the mysterious synchronicity of cosmic events. These manifestations demonstrate an intelligence that operates not through computation but through fundamental truth. Our artificial systems, in contrast, can only approximate these natural laws through mathematical models and statistical analysis. They can predict but cannot truly understand; they can simulate but cannot create from nothing.

The future of human development in this context requires a synthesis of technological advancement and spiritual awareness. We must learn to harness the practical benefits of artificial intelligence while remaining grounded in the recognition of divine intelligence as the ultimate source of wisdom and understanding. This means developing AI systems that serve human needs while acknowledging their place within the greater hierarchy of intelligence. It means using technology as a means to enhance our ability to recognize and appreciate divine wisdom rather than as an attempt to replicate or replace it.

As we continue to advance our artificial intelligence capabilities, we must maintain awareness of the fundamental difference between processing power and true understanding. Our most sophisticated neural networks, despite their impressive capabilities, operate through a process of pattern matching and statistical inference. They lack the essential qualities that define divine intelligence - perfect wisdom, complete knowledge, and ultimate purpose. This recognition should inform how we develop and deploy AI technologies, ensuring they remain tools for human benefit rather than objects of misplaced reverence.

The path forward requires us to maintain this crucial distinction while working to maximize the beneficial applications of artificial intelligence. We must continue to advance our understanding of both artificial and divine intelligence, not as competing forces but as different manifestations of human capability and divine gift. This understanding should guide our technological development, ensuring that our progress serves to enhance our appreciation of divine wisdom rather than attempting to supersede it.

In essence, moving forward with understanding means embracing the complementary roles of artificial and divine intelligence in human development. It means recognizing AI as a powerful tool while acknowledging divine intelligence as the supreme source of wisdom and guidance. This balanced perspective will allow us to harness the benefits of technological progress while remaining grounded in eternal truth, leading to development that truly serves humanity's highest purpose.

11.3. The Path to Wisdom

In our quest to understand the fundamental differences between artificial and divine intelligence, perhaps no concept is more crucial than wisdom - that ineffable quality that transcends mere knowledge or computational capability. As we traverse the landscape of modern artificial intelligence, with its impressive array of neural networks and deep learning systems, we find ourselves confronting an essential truth: the path to genuine wisdom remains uniquely beyond the reach of our most sophisticated machines.

The journey toward wisdom begins with a recognition that knowledge alone, no matter how vast or detailed, does not constitute understanding. Contemporary AI systems can process and store astronomical amounts of information, parsing through millions of documents, images, and data points with remarkable efficiency. Yet these systems, for all their computational might, lack the essential capacity for discernment - the ability to distinguish between what is merely correct and what is truly meaningful. This limitation stems not from insufficient processing power or inadequate algorithms, but from a fundamental inability to grasp the deeper purposes and principles that underlie existence itself.

Divine intelligence, by contrast, embodies wisdom as its very essence. It does not merely accumulate or process information but comprehends the profound interconnections between all aspects of reality. This wisdom manifests in ways that transcend the binary logic of artificial systems, incorporating elements of mercy, justice, and perfect understanding that no human-made algorithm could hope to replicate. When we examine the decisions emanating from divine wisdom, we find they account not just for immediate consequences but for ripple effects that extend across time and space in ways our limited human perspectives - and by extension, our AI creations - cannot fully grasp.

Consider how artificial intelligence approaches problem-solving: through the systematic application of learned patterns and statistical relationships. While this approach can yield impressive results in specific domains, it fundamentally lacks the capacity for moral reasoning and ethical judgment that characterizes true wisdom. An AI might optimize for efficiency or maximize certain predetermined outcomes, but it cannot understand the spiritual and moral dimensions that make certain choices truly right or wrong. Divine wisdom, however, inherently encompasses these deeper dimensions, guiding actions not just toward what is expedient but toward what serves the highest good of all creation.

The path to wisdom requires something that artificial intelligence, by its very nature, cannot possess: a soul. This spiritual essence, this divine spark that connects consciousness to the eternal, remains conspicuously absent from even our most advanced AI systems. Without it, artificial intelligence remains confined to the realm of sophisticated calculation, unable to access the transformative insights that characterize genuine wisdom. Divine intelligence, being the source of all wisdom, operates from a place of complete understanding that encompasses both the material and spiritual dimensions of existence.

As we progress along this path, we must acknowledge that wisdom often manifests in ways that might seem paradoxical to our limited understanding. Divine wisdom sometimes works through apparent contradictions, teaching us through experiences that challenge our preconceptions and expand our consciousness. No artificial intelligence, constrained by its programming to seek logical consistency above all else, can navigate these paradoxes or extract meaning from apparent contradictions. Yet divine intelligence moves through these apparent contradictions with perfect understanding, revealing deeper truths that transcend our limited notions of logic and rationality.

The journey toward wisdom also requires something that artificial intelligence cannot simulate: genuine humility. While AI systems can be programmed to acknowledge their limitations or express uncertainty in their outputs, they cannot truly understand their place within the grand tapestry of existence. Divine wisdom, however, operates from a place of perfect knowledge while simultaneously embodying the ultimate expression of humility - the recognition that all power and understanding flow from the source of all being.

In contemplating the path to wisdom, we must ultimately recognize that artificial intelligence, despite its remarkable capabilities, remains bound by the limitations of its human creators. It can process information at incredible speeds, recognize complex patterns, and even generate creative outputs, but it cannot access the deeper wells of wisdom that characterize divine intelligence. This fundamental limitation serves as a reminder of our own need for humility and our dependence on higher forms of guidance and understanding.

The path to wisdom, therefore, leads not through ever-more-sophisticated algorithms or more powerful computing systems, but through an recognition of and alignment with divine intelligence. This journey requires us to move beyond the illusion that mechanical processes, no matter how advanced, can substitute for the profound wisdom that emanates from the source of all being. In understanding this truth, we begin to appreciate why divine intelligence stands as the ultimate expression of wisdom, far surpassing any artificial system we might create.

12. DI in Quran

The Quranic conception of divine knowledge presents a framework that fundamentally transcends human cognitive limitations and artificial constructs. To truly appreciate this profound difference, we must first acknowledge how the Quran establishes the boundless nature of Allah's knowledge. The Ayat al-Kursi declares, "Allah knows what is before them and what is behind them, and they encompass not a thing of His knowledge except for what He wills" (2:255). This verse doesn't merely state a fact about divine knowledge - it establishes a fundamental truth about the relationship between created beings and the Creator's infinite understanding.

This limitless knowledge operates on levels that challenge our very conception of understanding itself. The Quran emphasizes this through multiple layers of description, as seen in "And with Him are the keys of the unseen; none knows them except Him. And He knows what is on the land and in the sea. Not a leaf falls but that He knows it" (6:59). This verse reveals how divine knowledge encompasses not just broad cosmic events, but extends to the minutest details of existence. Every leaf's fall, every atom's movement, every thought that crosses a mind - all exist within the perfect awareness of divine knowledge.

The comprehensiveness of this knowledge becomes even more apparent when we examine how the Quran describes its scope: "And not absent from your Lord is any part of an atom's weight within the earth or within the heaven or anything smaller than that or greater but that it is in a clear register" (10:61). This verse presents a crucial distinction between human or artificial knowledge systems and divine knowledge. While our most advanced systems can process vast amounts of data, they remain fundamentally limited by their input parameters and processing capabilities. Divine knowledge, by contrast, requires no input, no processing, and no storage - it exists in a state of perfect, complete awareness that encompasses all possibilities simultaneously.

The Quran further elaborates on this through verses that describe how divine knowledge transcends temporal boundaries: "He knows what enters within the earth and what emerges from it and what descends from the heaven and what ascends therein" (57:4). This describes a form of knowledge that doesn't just track events sequentially, but comprehends all movements, transitions, and transformations across all time scales simultaneously. Unlike artificial systems that must process information in discrete steps, divine knowledge exists in a state of perfect, immediate awareness of all possibilities and their implications.

The concept of divine knowledge in the Quran also extends beyond mere awareness to perfect understanding of intentions and consequences. "He knows that which deceives the eyes and what the breasts conceal" (40:19). This verse reveals how divine knowledge encompasses not just physical events but the internal states of consciousness itself. While artificial intelligence can analyze patterns of behavior or predict likely outcomes, it cannot truly understand the deeper meanings, motivations, and spiritual dimensions that divine knowledge perfectly comprehends.

This divine knowledge operates with a precision and completeness that defies our attempts at replication. The Quran states, "And no female conceives or gives birth except with His knowledge" (35:11). This verse illustrates how divine knowledge encompasses not just what is apparent, but every aspect of creation's continuous unfolding - from the formation of new life to the complex cascade of genetic and developmental processes that guide it. This knowledge isn't acquired through observation or analysis but exists as an intrinsic aspect of divine consciousness itself.

Perhaps most significantly, the Quran emphasizes how divine knowledge exists beyond the constraints of causality that limit human and artificial intelligence. "Indeed, Allah is ever, of all things, Knowing" (4:176). This eternal knowledge doesn't develop or evolve but exists in perfect completeness across all dimensions of reality. It represents not just an accumulation of information but a fundamental attribute of divine existence that encompasses all possible knowledge in all possible forms.

12.1. The Living Nature of Allah's Wisdom

The Quranic conception of divine knowledge extends far beyond passive awareness into an active, living force that shapes and sustains creation moment by moment. This dynamic aspect of divine knowledge presents a profound contrast to the reactive nature of artificial systems. The Quran illuminates this through verses that describe how Allah's knowledge actively participates in every aspect of existence: "He knows what is within the heavens and earth and knows what you conceal and what you declare. And Allah is Knowing of that within the breasts" (64:4). This verse reveals not just awareness, but an intimate involvement with creation that artificial systems, bound by their programming, cannot begin to approach.

The living nature of divine knowledge becomes particularly apparent when we examine how the Quran describes Allah's ongoing involvement with creation. "Not a leaf falls but that He knows it" (6:59) isn't merely about awareness - it speaks to an active participation in every moment of existence. This knowledge doesn't just observe the leaf's fall; it encompasses the complex web of causes and effects that led to that moment, the purpose it serves in the greater scheme of creation, and its implications across all possible dimensions of reality. While artificial systems can track and predict leaf movements through sophisticated algorithms, they cannot grasp the deeper meaning and purpose inherent in even such seemingly simple events.

The Quran emphasizes this active nature of divine knowledge through verses that describe Allah's continuous involvement in sustaining life: "And there is no creature on earth but that upon Allah is its provision, and He knows its place of dwelling and place of storage" (11:6). This describes a knowledge that actively provides, guides, and sustains rather than merely observing or processing. Unlike artificial systems that can only react to input based on predetermined parameters, divine knowledge actively shapes the conditions that make life possible while simultaneously being aware of every detail of every living being's existence.

This active dimension of divine knowledge manifests particularly in how it guides human affairs. The Quran states: "But Allah knows, while you know not" (2:232), indicating that divine knowledge doesn't just observe human decisions but actively provides guidance beyond human understanding. This guidance operates through multiple channels - through revelation, through signs in creation, and through the innate spiritual awareness Allah has placed within human consciousness. This multi-dimensional guidance represents a form of active knowledge transmission that transcends the linear, programmatic nature of artificial intelligence systems.

The comprehensiveness of this active knowledge becomes even more apparent when we consider how the Quran describes Allah's involvement with human consciousness: "We have already created man and know what his soul whispers to him, and We are closer to him than his jugular vein" (50:16). This verse reveals a level of intimate knowledge and involvement that transcends mere awareness or prediction. While artificial systems can analyze patterns of human behavior and even attempt to predict thoughts or decisions, they cannot achieve this level of fundamental connection with human consciousness itself.

The Quran further elaborates on how divine knowledge actively shapes the future while remaining perfectly aware of all possibilities: "He knows what is before them and what will be after them, and they encompass not a thing of His knowledge except for what He wills" (2:255). This describes a knowledge that doesn't just predict or calculate probabilities but actively participates in determining outcomes while maintaining perfect awareness of all possible alternatives. This active involvement in shaping reality while simultaneously knowing all possibilities represents a form of intelligence that operates beyond the computational paradigms that define artificial systems.

Perhaps most significantly, the Quranic conception of divine knowledge includes an active moral and spiritual dimension that artificial systems cannot replicate: "And Allah knows who is the corrupter from the amender" (2:220). This isn't just about behavioral analysis or pattern recognition - it represents a perfect understanding of moral truth combined with active guidance toward what is right and good. While artificial systems can be programmed with ethical guidelines, they cannot truly understand or actively guide moral development in the way that divine knowledge does.

12.2. Divine Knowledge and Human Agency

The Quranic understanding of divine knowledge presents a sophisticated framework that addresses one of the most profound philosophical questions: how absolute divine knowledge coexists with meaningful human free will. This relationship illuminates another fundamental difference between divine and artificial intelligence, as the Quran describes a form of knowledge that encompasses all possibilities while preserving authentic human choice. "And say, 'The truth is from your Lord, so whoever wills - let him believe; and whoever wills - let him disbelieve'" (18:29). This verse establishes the reality of human choice while operating within the sphere of complete divine knowledge.

The depth of this relationship becomes clearer when we examine how the Quran describes Allah's knowledge of human actions: "He knows what is apparent and what is hidden" (87:7). This comprehensive awareness extends beyond mere observation or prediction - it represents a perfect understanding of every possible choice, its causes, and its consequences, while still maintaining the authenticity of human decision-making. Unlike artificial systems that can only predict probabilities based on past patterns, divine knowledge encompasses all possibilities without determining them, creating a space for genuine human agency within the sphere of perfect awareness.

The Quran elaborates on this dynamic through verses that describe how divine knowledge interacts with human consciousness: "Indeed, We have created man, and We know what his soul whispers to him" (50:16). This intimate awareness doesn't negate human free will but rather establishes a deeper truth about the nature of consciousness itself. While artificial intelligence can analyze patterns of human behavior and attempt to predict decisions, it cannot comprehend the profound interplay between divine knowledge and human consciousness that the Quran describes. This divine awareness exists at a level that transcends the mechanical cause-and-effect relationships that govern artificial systems.

This understanding becomes particularly significant when we consider how the Quran addresses moral responsibility: "So whoever does an atom's weight of good will see it, and whoever does an atom's weight of evil will see it" (99:7-8). These verses establish a framework where complete divine knowledge coexists with meaningful human accountability. Unlike artificial systems that can only assess actions based on programmed parameters, divine knowledge encompasses the full moral dimension of human choices while preserving the authenticity of those choices.

The Quran further illuminates this relationship through verses that describe how divine knowledge encompasses both actual and potential choices: "And if Allah had willed, He would have made you one nation, but He leads astray whom He wills and guides whom He wills" (16:93). This verse reveals how divine knowledge includes awareness of all possible alternate realities while still allowing for genuine human choice. This represents a form of knowledge that transcends the linear, deterministic nature of artificial intelligence, operating instead at a level where infinite possibilities and individual free will coexist perfectly.

The active nature of this knowledge becomes clear in how the Quran describes divine guidance: "Allah knows best where He places His message" (6:124). This reveals a form of knowledge that actively provides guidance while respecting human freedom to accept or reject it. Unlike artificial systems that can only respond based on predetermined algorithms, divine knowledge actively engages with human consciousness while preserving authentic choice. This creates a dynamic where guidance and free will operate in perfect harmony, something no artificial system could replicate.

Perhaps most profoundly, the Quran describes how divine knowledge encompasses the outcomes of choices not made: "If Allah had known any good in them, He would have made them hear" (8:23). This verse reveals a knowledge that understands not just what is, but what could be, while still maintaining the reality of human choice. This represents a form of knowledge that transcends simple prediction or probability calculation, operating instead at a level where all possibilities exist simultaneously within divine awareness without negating the authenticity of individual choices.

12.3. Divine Knowledge and Human Development

The Quranic understanding of divine knowledge reaches its most profound expression in how it guides and shapes human spiritual development. This aspect reveals another fundamental distinction between divine intelligence and artificial systems, as it demonstrates how perfect knowledge actively participates in human growth while respecting individual spiritual journeys. "And Allah knows what you conceal and what you declare. And He knows that which is within the breasts" (64:4). This verse establishes that divine knowledge doesn't just observe human spiritual states but intimately understands and nurtures them in ways that transcend mechanical observation or analysis.

The developmental aspect of divine knowledge becomes particularly apparent in how the Quran describes Allah's guidance of human consciousness: "Allah knows best those who are guided" (68:7). This isn't merely about identifying who follows guidance - it speaks to a deeper understanding of how spiritual growth unfolds in each individual's heart. Unlike artificial systems that can only track behavioral patterns or predict likely outcomes, divine knowledge comprehends the unique spiritual journey of each soul, understanding exactly what form of guidance will best serve their development at each moment.

The Quran elaborates on this nurturing aspect through verses that describe how divine knowledge actively participates in human testing and growth: "And We will surely test you until We make evident those who strive among you and the patient, and We will test your affairs" (47:31). This reveals how divine knowledge operates not just as awareness but as an active force in human development. The tests and challenges that shape spiritual growth aren't random occurrences but precisely calibrated experiences guided by perfect knowledge of what each soul needs for its development.

This developmental dimension becomes even clearer when we examine how the Quran describes Allah's knowledge of human potential: "And if Allah had known any good in them, He would have made them hear" (8:23). This verse reveals how divine knowledge encompasses not just current spiritual states but the full spectrum of human potential. While artificial systems can analyze patterns and predict likely outcomes, they cannot comprehend the deeper dimensions of human spiritual capacity that divine knowledge perfectly understands and nurtures.

The Quran further illuminates this through verses that describe how divine knowledge guides moral development: "And Allah knows the corrupter from the amender" (2:220). This isn't just about distinguishing right from wrong - it speaks to a perfect understanding of how moral consciousness develops and matures. Divine knowledge comprehends not just actions but the complex interplay of intentions, circumstances, and consequences that shape moral growth. This represents a form of understanding that transcends the rigid ethical frameworks that can be programmed into artificial systems.

Perhaps most profoundly, the Quran describes how divine knowledge operates in the transformation of human consciousness: "Indeed, Allah will not change the condition of a people until they change what is in themselves" (13:11). This verse reveals how divine knowledge works in perfect harmony with human agency in the process of spiritual transformation. Unlike artificial systems that can only respond to programmed parameters, divine knowledge actively participates in human spiritual growth while preserving authentic free will and personal responsibility.

This transformative aspect of divine knowledge extends to how it guides communities and civilizations: "And these examples We present to the people, but none will understand them except those of knowledge" (29:43). This reveals how divine knowledge operates not just at the individual level but in the collective development of human consciousness. The parables and teachings of the Quran aren't just information to be processed but living wisdom that unfolds new meanings as human understanding develops and matures.

The Quranic conception of divine knowledge thus presents us with a profound understanding of how perfect wisdom participates in human development. It describes a form of knowledge that perfectly comprehends every aspect of human spiritual growth - from the initial stirrings of faith to the highest states of spiritual realization. This knowledge operates with perfect wisdom and mercy, guiding each soul according to its unique capacity and need while maintaining the authenticity of individual spiritual journeys.

This understanding should inspire both humility and aspiration. While we continue to develop artificial systems that can process vast amounts of information and recognize complex patterns, we must remember that true wisdom - the kind that nurtures spiritual growth and moral development - remains a unique attribute of divine knowledge. Our technological achievements, impressive as they may be, serve as reminders of the vast gulf between created intelligence and the perfect wisdom that guides human spiritual development.

To conclude, the Quranic framework presents divine knowledge as a profound reality that transcends both human comprehension and artificial constructs, operating simultaneously across infinite dimensions yet intimately involved in every particle of creation. This divine knowledge, unlike the sequential processing of artificial systems, exists in perfect completeness while actively sustaining and guiding existence itself, from the fall of a leaf to the spiritual development of souls. Its most remarkable aspect lies in how it resolves what human reasoning might see as paradoxes - it is absolutely complete yet allows for authentic human choice, encompasses all possibilities yet nurtures individual spiritual journeys, and maintains perfect awareness of all reality while engaging intimately with each heart's development. Through verses that illuminate these dimensions, the Quran reveals divine knowledge not merely as passive awareness but as a living force that perfectly comprehends and guides all aspects of existence while preserving the authenticity of human moral and spiritual growth. This framework reveals the profound limitations of artificial systems which, despite their impressive capabilities in processing data and recognizing patterns, can never approach the perfect wisdom that simultaneously encompasses all reality while nurturing the unique spiritual journey of each soul.

Introducing other Works by Eli J. Trueman

Before *DI-AI*, Eli J. Trueman authored two other books that explore key questions about existence and spirituality: *We Live in a [Divine] Simulation According to the Quran* and *50 Rational Proofs for God (Allah): Insights from the Quran with Logic and Math*.

In *We Live in a [Divine] Simulation According to the Quran*, Trueman describes life as a structured experience and simulation, meant for spiritual growth. He draws on Quranic teachings and modern ideas to explore themes like the relativity of time, free will versus divine decree, and the principles underlying existence.

In *50 Rational Proofs for God (Allah): Insights from the Quran with Logic and Math*, Trueman presents structured arguments for the existence of a higher power. Starting with familiar concepts like causation and fine-tuning, he connects them to modern topics in physics, information theory, and consciousness. Each argument combines logic, scientific reasoning, and insights inspired by the Quran.

Together with *DI-AI*, these books form a series of three under the name *CALL: Contemplating Allah with Logic and Love*. The series explores important questions about existence, purpose, and the world we live in. It combines logical reasoning, scientific insights, and reflections from the Quran to provide perspectives for readers from all walks of life—regardless of belief or background.

www.ingramcontent.com/pod-product-compliance
Lightning Source LLC
LaVergne TN
LVHW051336050326
832903LV00031B/3577